BUTTERFLIES

OF THE

SOUTHWEST

BUTTERFLIES

OF THE

SOUTHWEST

JIM P. BROCK

RIO NUEVO PUBLISHERS
TUCSON, ARIZONA

Rio Nuevo Publishers®
P.O. Box 5250, Tucson, Arizona 85703-0250
(520) 623-9558, www.rionuevo.com

On the front cover: Gulf Fritillary (main image); Monarch, Black Swallowtail,
Queen (left to right). On page 2: Sonora Blue; page 5: Goatweed Leafwing; page 12:
Pipevine Swallowtail.

Library of Congress Cataloging-in-Publication Data

Brock, James P.
Butterflies of the Southwest / Jim P. Brock.
     p. cm.
Includes index.
ISBN 978-1-933855-15-8
  1. Butterflies—Southwestern States—Identification. I. Title.
QL551.S87B76 2008
595.78'90979—dc22

                          2007051257

Design: Karen Schober, Seattle, Washington

Printed in Korea.
10 9 8 7 6 5 4 3 2 1

INTRODUCTION

· · · · · ·

BUTTERFLIES ARE AMONG THE WORLD'S MOST BEAUTIFUL CREATURES, and they grow in popularity with each new generation. We celebrate them, study them, watch them, take their pictures, and feel a sense of wonder in their company. And we aren't their first admirers—butterflies have been a part of human culture for centuries. They exist in the art and sculptures of early civilizations. But they have been around even longer, co-evolving with flowering plants for millions of years—cultivating a relationship so intimate that most butterflies depend upon plants for survival.

Butterflies (along with moths) are insects in the order Lepidoptera, meaning "scale-winged." They get their beautiful colors from thousands of tiny scales attached to their wings. Like all insects they have six legs, a pair of compound eyes, and a pair of sensory antennae. Butterflies have a segmented body supported by an exoskeleton, a hard outer covering made mostly of a substance called chitin. The body is divided into a head, thorax, and abdomen. A pair of forewings and a pair of hindwings attached to the thorax enable them to fly. The mouth consists of a double straw-like tube known as a proboscis, through which they get nourishment—primarily nectar from flowers.

Some species prefer rotting fruit, tree sap, carrion, dung, or salt taken from mud. These alternative nutrients are also used in mating and are especially sought by male butterflies, which are often found sipping at mud in numbers. These congregations are called "puddle parties," and although usually limited to a few individuals, they sometimes number in the hundreds.

Butterflies are cold-blooded, meaning they require warm temperatures to become active. To do this, most species bask with their wings wide open to the sun on cool mornings. Butterflies that rest with wings completely closed simply angle their wings to catch the maximum amount of warmth from the sun's rays. Likewise, to cool down, butterflies either close their wings or reverse their position. Temperatures generally need to be 60 degrees Fahrenheit or warmer before they can fly.

In order to survive extended periods of cold, or of hot temperatures and drought, butterflies (and other insects) enter "diapause." This state is similar to hibernation, except that no growth occurs during diapause, and reproduction is suspended. For most southwestern butterfly species, the timing of diapause is genetically predetermined. Although for most species diapause occurs during the colder months of winter ("overwintering"), some species may delay growth and reproduction during the dry, early summer. (See the "Life Cycles" section below for more on diapause.)

Once on the wing (after their emergence as adults), butterflies respond to their environment through sensory input. They use their antennae, legs and feet, eyes, proboscis, and even their abdomens to find flowers, mates, or hostplants. Their behavior in response to various stimuli is inherently instinctual. However, butterflies display some degree of learning from experience; they are able to learn to discern colors and shapes, for example. It is difficult to know what a butterfly actually sees. However, it has been proven that butterflies see a broader spectrum of color than humans, including ultraviolet colors that are reflected by other butterflies and flowers. This aids them in finding not only nectar but also mates.

Most butterflies are herbivores and occur everywhere that plants are found. We often encounter them, although most of us rarely take the time to try to get to know them. Little is known about their day-to-day lives, for they are reluctant to reveal their secrets. Researchers spend long hours in both the field and the lab, trying to unlock these mysteries, but many discoveries are actually made by dedicated amateurs.

Fortunately, more amateurs get interested in butterflies every year. Butterfly clubs and organizations are now found throughout the country and offer a great venue for socializing and making new friends. They also offer field trips, identification and photography seminars, and up-to-date information on local butterfly events.

This book is intended as an introduction for those with a general interest in butterflies, as well as a guide for butterfly enthusiasts.

Life Cycles

The life cycle of the butterfly is one of nature's great miracles. The transformation from caterpillar to butterfly has inspired, captivated, and amazed for centuries. However, the transformation does not start with the caterpillar. It starts with the egg—the first of four stages in the life cycle of a butterfly.

EGG Butterfly eggs are stored in the abdomen of the female and are fertilized by the male. Before laying eggs, the female must locate the proper "host" plant by touching leaves with her feet. Some butterflies are very particular and can use only a family of closely related plants, which will provide food for the emerging caterpillars. Others are polyphagous, meaning their caterpillars can eat a variety of plants from many plant families. Most eggs are laid directly on or very near the hostplant and attached with a glue-like substance produced in the female's abdomen.

A female lays anywhere from a dozen to more than a hundred eggs during her short lifetime. Eggs are laid singly, in small clusters, or in masses of a hundred or more, depending primarily on the species. Butterfly eggs are vulnerable to weather, disease, mold, predators, and parasites, and most do not survive to become caterpillars.

The eggs come in various shapes, sizes, and colors. Swallowtails, brushfoots, and skippers lay round eggs. Those of the sulphurs and whites are spindle-shaped. Gossamer wings lay round, flattened eggs that look like sea urchins. Some eggs are ribbed or covered with tiny indentations, while others are relatively smooth. Most butterfly eggs hatch within a few days, although some hairstreaks diapause in this stage.

CATERPILLAR The second stage of a butterfly's development is the caterpillar—a growth stage that has a large hand in determining the eventual size of the adult. Caterpillars have chewing mouthparts and emerge from the egg by eating through the shell. Some eat the entire eggshell, while other caterpillars begin to feed by nibbling on tender leaves, flowers, or seeds. As the tiny caterpillar increases in size it outgrows its skin (exoskeleton). As growth continues the skin splits open, revealing a new, larger skin underneath. This process is termed a molt, and most caterpillars undergo from three to five molts during their development; the periods between molts are called "instars." The colors and patterns of some caterpillars change dramatically following later molts.

The length of time needed for development varies from species to species and is primarily influenced by season and weather. Most caterpillars feed for only two to three weeks. Many southwestern butterflies diapause as caterpillars, by crawling into curled leaves or other debris at the base of the hostplant. When feeding is complete, the caterpillar usually crawls away to a safe, protected place to pupate.

PUPA Upon reaching a secure spot, the caterpillar attaches itself to a support with silk and prepares to pupate, shedding its skin one last time. Some caterpillars hang upside down, while others rest horizontally or vertically. After a day or so the skin is shed and the pupa (or chrysalis) is revealed. The exoskeleton is now a hard, seemingly lifeless outer shell. Some chrysalids have bright colors and markings, but most are camouflaged to avoid detection by predators. Unlike moths, most butterflies do not have a cocoon or silken case surrounding the pupa; however, some skippers make cocoons or cocoon-like nests out of leaves and other debris.

Inside the pupa the tissues and structures of the caterpillar are undergoing the amazing transformation into an adult butterfly. For small butterflies this process may take only one week. For swallowtails and other large species it takes about two weeks. Many butterflies diapause as pupae and are able to delay the transformation process for months or even years.

ADULT The adult butterfly emerges from the pupa shell. At first its wings are soft and curled up. Fluid is pumped into the wing veins and they unfurl, displaying the adult butterfly in its final form. Although adult butterflies feed at flowers, mud, rotting fruit, etc., they do not grow.

MATING An adult butterfly's main purpose is to mate and secure the survival of its species. Male butterflies go to great lengths to find females. Some seek mountain summits, while others relentlessly patrol canyon bottoms. Males of some species set up specific territories, which are small areas with strategic perches. A number of species may be predictably located by these behaviors, which will vary as to their duration and the time of day they occur.

While it may be love at first sight for a male and female butterfly, it's the exchange of scent or pheromones specific to that species that seals the deal. Butterflies actually have poor distance vision, so males need to be close to a potential mate before courtship begins and its pheromones are released. Some males court females with an aerial display. Others land near the female and attempt to make tactile contact. If the female is receptive, the male uses a pair of organs known as claspers at the tip of its abdomen to grasp the female, and copulation takes place. This may last for minutes or hours. During copulation one or the other butterfly is able to fly, with the mate hanging underneath.

Unreceptive or mated females often flutter or display their wings to reject unwanted advances. Both the males and females of most butterflies can mate more than once in their short lifetimes. Some brushfoots and sulphurs diapause as adult butterflies; this occurs mostly during cold winter months, and though they may be seen on the wing during periods of warm weather, they will not breed during this time.

LIFE SPAN Most adult butterflies live, on the average, only one to two weeks. Smaller butterflies may last only five or six days; larger ones sometimes live up to three weeks. Butterflies live longer in cooler months, since they tend to be less active with shorter daylight hours and cooler overall temperatures. Conversely, their lives are shortened by the hot temperatures of summer.

Desert butterflies are well adapted to where they live, and some species live many months or years in diapause. Diapause may occur in any one of the four stages of development, depending on the species involved and to some degree where it lives. For instance, the Soapberry Hairstreak lays its eggs on the soapberry tree during its flight in June. The eggs do not hatch until the following April, when the soapberry trees offer them fresh, tender foliage. Thus, the first-stage caterpillar is already about ten months old when it starts to eat. It takes the caterpillar two weeks to feed and another week for the pupa to develop. When the adult emerges, the butterfly is around eleven months old.

The Sagebrush Checkerspot lays its eggs on asters in May. In a few days the eggs hatch, and the caterpillars feed for a couple of weeks before going into diapause prior to summer. There they will sit until the new growth appears the following spring. Following dry winters they are capable of extending their diapause another year and possibly longer. It is quite conceivable that one could happen upon an adult Sagebrush Checkerspot that is two or more years old, although most of its life has inactively passed in diapause.

Most desert butterflies can go into diapause during periods of drought. The timing and amount of rainfall is critical for their survival. Some species, such as the Desert Orangetip, diapause as a pupa. They have been known to live as a pupa for up to six years. Their caterpillars eat only spring annuals, so diapause is extended following winters that fail to germinate their precious hostplants.

Mourning Cloaks, other brushfoots, and most sulphurs diapause as adults and may be seen flying on warm days during the middle of winter. These are some of our longest-lived adult butterflies, although most of their time is spent resting in a protective place. Mourning Cloaks are known to live up to ten months as adults.

Butterfly Color

Butterfly colors and patterns endear them to us, though this is not nature's intention. Nature has blessed each species with a unique design that aids them in mating and survival. Perhaps this is their *real* attraction, for they reveal their genetic history on their wings, a history still in progress that is studied by many.

A butterfly's wing is essentially a clear membrane covered with thousands of tiny scales aligned much like shingles on a roof. Each scale has its own color and is attached to the wing by a tiny stalk. Wing colors such as black, brown, gray, red, orange, yellow, and white are created by *pigmented* scales, whereas the blues, purples, greens, and silvers found on butterflies are caused by *structural* scales, which reflect light at different angles and wavelengths, causing varying degrees of iridescence. Many butterflies, such as the Variable Checkerspot, have only pigmented scales, while others, like the Gulf Fritillary, have both pigmented and structural scales.

Butterflies may also have specialized scales that emit pheromones used for mating. On the males of some skippers and some hairstreaks, these scales are easily visible as a sharply defined black mark, known as a stigma, on the upper forewing. Some male spread-wing skippers contain sex scales in a small sac known as a costal fold along the top of the forewing near the head. Monarchs and Queens have small scent pouches easily visible on the hindwing.

Color and pattern play a major role in mate location. For those species that look identical to our eyes, ultraviolet reflectance and pheromones unique to those species are used to a greater degree. Males and females of most species look similar, although the sexes can look very different, as in the case of the Mexican Pine White.

Color and pattern on the upper surface of a butterfly are usually very different as compared with the under surface. Most butterflies roost with their wings closed, and thus, they tend to be camouflaged because of their underside markings. On top, the pattern is often bolder, with brighter colors to either warn predators of distastefulness or to aid in thermoregulation.

Migration

Compared with birds, most butterflies are generally sedentary creatures, rarely wandering far from their birthplace. The Monarch is the closet thing to a true migratory butterfly. Their massive fall flights to overwintering sites in Mexico and along the West Coast of the U.S. (where they go into reproductive diapause) are legendary. However, unlike birds, the same individuals do not return to their place of origin.

So, the term *migration,* when referring to butterflies, does not accurately define what they actually do. A good number of our Southwest butterflies undergo movements or dispersals of some degree in a particular direction, but for most species these flights are unpredictable; they often go unnoticed, and they eventually die out without establishing permanent new colonies.

One species that undergoes massive directional movements is the Painted Lady. Although these flights don't occur every year, individuals often number in the millions and cover vast areas of the desert Southwest. Sometimes there are so many Painted Ladies crossing our highways that they become a nuisance to travelers and consequently attract media attention. These individuals emanate from Mexico and move generally to the northwest. No return flights have been noted, although it may be that some individuals indeed return southward in the fall but do so virtually unnoticed.

Other species undergo directional flights into the U.S. Southwest from Mexico. In some years these movements contain millions of individuals. Cloudless Sulphurs and Lyside Sulphurs are two examples of these. Summer rains appear to precipitate these flights, and both species appear to be attempting to expand their range. Cloudless Sulphurs are at least temporarily successful at this before perishing with winter freezes. Lysides face a more difficult challenge, as their suitable hostplants do not occur naturally in the Southwest. Indeed, return flights of thousands have been noted.

Some butterflies, such as the Red Admiral, Reakirt's Blue, and Mourning Cloak, undergo elevational movements. To avoid freezing winters at high elevations, adults descend in the fall to warmer lowland refuges; then their offspring return the following spring.

Perhaps even the most localized and sedentary butterfly species have the ability to disperse, meaning in any given brood at least some individuals wander away from their birthplace either by error or deliberately to establish new colonies. Individuals discovered far from their normal haunts are often newsworthy among butterfly enthusiasts, although for the butterfly it may be just another strategy for survival.

Butterfly or Moth?

What is the difference between a butterfly and a moth? The answer is not as simple as saying moths fly at night and butterflies fly during the day. There are many brightly colored day-flying moths to confuse the beginning observer, and some tropical butterflies fly well after dark.

The classification of moths and butterflies is based upon physiological differences; thus, they are separated into different superfamilies. There are numerous superfamilies of moths. Butterflies are in the superfamily Papilionoidea. One can visually distinguish between butterflies and moths by the shape of the antennae. Butterfly antennae are clubbed or swollen at the tip. Most moth antennae are feathery, threadlike, or notched along the edge. In addition, the forewing and hindwing of a moth are joined by a hooked structure known as a frenulum, a feature lacking on butterflies.

SPECIES ACCOUNTS
· · · · · ·

FOR THIS BOOK, the region defined as the Southwest includes desert areas from southeastern California and adjacent Nevada eastward through Arizona and New Mexico to western Texas. Included in this region are the biologically rich "sky islands" (mountaintops with isolated ecosystems) of Arizona and adjacent New Mexico.

In the United States, the butterfly diversity of the Southwest is second only to that of the subtropical regions of southern Texas. Worldwide there are six families of butterflies, and all six families and numerous subfamilies are represented in the Southwest. Of the nearly 300 species recorded in the region, 141 are treated herein, most of them common and familiar. A few influx species, part-time residents, and rarities are also included.

The information presented includes flight period (when the species is in its "adult" phase), size, habitat, behavior, hostplants used in the Southwest (there may be additional hostplants for some of these species in other areas), and the butterfly's range. In some cases identification tips are included—but not all butterflies are identifiable, even with book in hand. Butterflies are quite variable and subject to the rigors of insect life. It is not uncommon to find butterflies missing most of their scales or missing field marks due to wing damage. While this may hamper identification, it should not prevent one from enjoying them.

The butterflies presented in this book are arranged by family. Members of each family are then arranged in taxonomic order. However, butterfly taxonomy is still quite fluid and subject to frequent rearranging, especially at the genus and species level.

At present there is no standardized official list of common English names for butterflies as there is for birds. Some common butterflies have more than one English name. To simplify things, the English names used in this book generally follow the *NABA Checklist & English Names of North American Butterflies* (second edition, 2001), compiled by the North American Butterfly Association (NABA). This list is currently the standard among most butterfly enthusiasts.

Some butterfly species vary in color and pattern from region to region. These species are given subspecific (meaning subspecies-specific) names in many cases, and many of our butterflies have these designations. For simplification, the scientific names used in this book include only the genus and species. Subspecific names are left for the more serious student and may be found in more scientific treatments.

Please note that seasons vary by elevation and latitude, so "spring" may mean some time earlier in warmer areas and later in cool er ones.

SWALLOWTAILS (FAMILY PAPILIONIDAE)

These are our largest (ranging in size from about 2½ to 4½ inches in wingspan) and most conspicuous butterflies, usually with one or more tails on the hindwing. Swallowtails are strong fliers and avidly visit flowers and mud. Most have caterpillars that resemble bird droppings, especially in their early instars. Swallowtails diapause as chrysalids.

Pipevine Swallowtail *(Battus philenor)*

FAMILY: Papilionidae (Swallowtails)
RANGE: AZ to west TX, mainly absent west of
    Colorado River (also across southern U.S. to
    East Coast)
ADULT FLIGHT SEASON: spring to fall
HOSTPLANT: pipevine
WINGSPAN: 2½–3¼ inches

Pipevine Swallowtails are widespread and common, occupying a variety of habitats including grasslands, foothills, higher deserts, and city gardens. Adults occur mainly from spring to fall and may wander well up into the mountains, far beyond their hostplant colonies. Males are a frequent sight on desert hilltops, where they seek mates.

The brilliant blue, black, and orange colors of this butterfly are pleasing to the eye, but more important, the colors warn predators of distastefulness. The caterpillars feed on pipevine, a plant containing poisonous alkaloids that render them toxic to most predators. This toxicity persists in all stages of Pipevine Swallowtail, all of which are brightly colored. The similar-looking Red-spotted Purple (see page 50) gains some degree of protection as a mimic of the Pipevine Swallowtail.

Black Swallowtail *(Papilio polyxenes)*

FAMILY: Papilionidae (Swallowtails)
RANGE: CA to TX (also across U.S. to East
    Coast)
ADULT FLIGHT SEASON: spring to fall
HOSTPLANT: cultivated and weedy members
    of the parsley family, turpentine broom
WINGSPAN: 2½–3½ inches

Male

Black Swallowtails are a common sight across most of North America. In the Southwest they may be more common in areas of cultivation and gardens, but they also range well up into the mountains. The males are black with yellow bands and marginal spots, the females mostly black and blue. In western deserts most adults are predominantly yellow. Males patrol foothill and mountain summits to locate females. The brightly colored caterpillars can be a pest in herb gardens.

Female

Western Tiger Swallowtail *(Papilio rutulus)*

FAMILY: Papilionidae (Swallowtails)
RANGE: CA to extreme west TX sky islands (also in most of the West)
ADULT FLIGHT SEASON: summer
HOSTPLANT: quaking aspen, California sycamore, and others
WINGSPAN: 3–3⅝ inches

A look-alike to the Two-tailed Swallowtail (see next entry), this butterfly has only a single tail on each hindwing and thicker black tiger stripes. Despite their similarity, the habitats of these two species barely overlap, with Western Tigers restricted to higher mountain meadows and aspen groves above 7,000 feet, and to the sycamore-lined canyons along the extreme western desert around Anza-Borrego Desert State Park and vicinity in California. Adults are fond of flowers, and males can be found around mud. Mt. Graham in Arizona is a great place to see this species.

Two-tailed Swallowtail *(Papilio multicaudata)*

FAMILY: Papilionidae (Swallowtails)

RANGE: AZ to west TX, absent from lower
desert regions in CA and western AZ
(found in most mountain regions west of
Great Plains)

ADULT FLIGHT SEASON: spring to fall

HOSTPLANT: velvet ash, hop tree, wild cherry

WINGSPAN: 3½–4½ inches

From spring to fall, even the most casual of
observers may notice this grand butterfly soaring down a Southwest canyon. Two-taileds are found primarily in mid-elevation canyons and riparian woodlands, occasionally venturing into cities and towns. Males often stop at mud for salt and after some time may be easily approached. Both sexes attend flowers, especially thistles. Named for the two tail-like projections on the hindwing, this is the largest butterfly in the Southwest. Declared the official state butterfly of Arizona in 2001.

Giant Swallowtail *(Papilio cresphontes)*

FAMILY: Papilionidae (Swallowtails)

RANGE: CA to TX (also across southern U.S. to
FL)

ADULT FLIGHT SEASON: spring to fall

HOSTPLANT: citrus, hop trees

WINGSPAN: 3½–4 inches

This large, conspicuous swallowtail is a very
familiar sight in Southwest cities and gardens
where citrus plantings occur. It is not nearly as
common in more natural habitats. Giant Swallowtails are delightful creatures to attract to one's gar-
den and are especially fond of lantana flowers. Males are attracted to mud. The caterpillars are sometimes considered a pest on citrus, although most damage is restricted to fresh sucker growth.

WHITES AND SULPHURS (FAMILY PIERIDAE)

Whites are generally small (1 to 2 inches in wingspan) white, yellow, or orange butterflies with black markings. Some have lovely green, marbled undersides. In flight, their bright colors are a stark contrast to various habitats; consequently they are easily noticed, although adults rarely stop for any length of time, which can frustrate the most patient of observers. Their flight is direct, fairly erratic, and usually close to the ground. Adults will perch with wings closed or partially open. The caterpillars are mostly green or painted in purple, white, yellow, or maroon, with tiny raised bumps, and sparsely covered with short hairs. Most whites diapause as chrysalids.

Sulphurs are usually yellow, orange, red, white, or light green. They range in size from 1 to 3 inches in wingspan. Larger species are strong fliers and are conspicuous in flight. Smaller species fly erratically, close to the ground. Adults almost never perch with wings open. Sulphur caterpillars are also mostly green, or painted in blue, white, yellow, or maroon, with tiny raised bumps. Most sulphurs diapause as adults.

Mexican Pine White *(Neophasia terlooii)*

Female

FAMILY: Pieridae (Whites and Sulphurs)
RANGE: southeast AZ, southwest NM
ADULT FLIGHT SEASON: June to Nov.
HOSTPLANT: ponderosa and other pines
WINGSPAN: 1¾–2⅜ inches

This rarity of sky-island coniferous forests is well worth seeking. It is unique for a "white" in that, unlike the males, the females are bright orange. Also, unlike most butterflies, Mexican Pine Whites spend most of their time lazily flitting high up in the canopy of the pines that also serve as the hostplant for their caterpillars. However, on some days adults will descend en masse, allowing good, close looks. Females lay their eggs in rows on pine needles. Adults occur

Male

from June to November but are most common in October.

Checkered White *(Pontia protodice)*

FAMILY: Pieridae (Whites and Sulphurs)
RANGE: CA to TX (also most of the U.S.)
ADULT FLIGHT SEASON: year-round
HOSTPLANT: London rocket, pepper grass,
    and other exotic and native mustards
WINGSPAN: 1¼–2 inches

Few butterflies are as adaptable as the Checkered White. Their ability to utilize a

variety of both native and exotic mustard plants gives them the flexibility to choose fertile habitats over those with less favorable conditions and to move freely about at all elevations. Males readily congregate on hilltops to search for females. Both sexes visit flowers. On the dorsal surface, males are mostly white, while females are more heavily checkered with black. The hindwing underside varies in the amount of yellow-brown veining. Springtime individuals that have diapaused as pupae are generally smaller and darker than their offspring and can be easily confused with Spring Whites (see next entry). Adults can be found year-round but are usually scarce in areas of drought.

Spring White *(Pontia sisymbrii)*

FAMILY: Pieridae (Whites and Sulphurs)
RANGE: CA to west TX (also western U.S.)
ADULT FLIGHT SEASON: spring
HOSTPLANT: rock cress, tumble mustard,
    and others
WINGSPAN: 1¼–1⅜ inches

This lovely and rather uncommon white is found mainly in hilly mid-elevation habitats (above 2,000 feet) but sometimes ranges up into higher mountains. While rock cress appears to be a contributing factor as to where populations of this butterfly occur, they'll also use other mustards. The sexes are similar and usually white, although females have more black markings on the upper side and may also be cream or light yellow. Adults primarily patrol up and down canyons and across hillsides, only occasionally stopping at flowers, where visitation is brief (and getting good looks takes patience). Males are best found seeking females on mid-elevation hilltops but are more approachable when encountered at mud.

Cabbage White *(Pieris rapae)*

FAMILY: Pieridae (Whites and Sulphurs)
RANGE: CA to TX, mainly absent in
    extremely dry desert regions (also present
    in most of the U.S.)
ADULT FLIGHT SEASON: nearly year-round
HOSTPLANT: cabbage, nasturtium, capers,
    etc.
WINGSPAN: about 1½ inches

Since their accidental introduction into North America from Europe in the mid-1800s, Cabbage Whites have infiltrated cities, fields, and gardens across the entire continent. Common and widespread through most of their range, they are primarily restricted to gardens and moist natural areas in the Southwest. In large numbers they are considered a pest of cabbage and related plants. Both adults are white, the males with one black spot on the forewing, the female with two. The hindwings underneath vary from creamy yellow to white. Both sexes visit flowers, and adults are on the wing most of the year.

Desert Marble *(Euchloe lotta)*

FAMILY: Pieridae (Whites and Sulphurs)
RANGE: CA to west TX (also western U.S.)
ADULT FLIGHT SEASON: spring
HOSTPLANT: tansy mustard, lacepod, and
    other native mustards
WINGSPAN: 1–1½ inches

Marbles are small, white, spring-flying butterflies represented in North America by a half dozen or so species. They are named for the yellowish-green marbled pattern found underneath the hindwing. At rest, this pattern allows them to disappear into the backround to avoid predators. Following wet winters the Desert Marble may be rather common. Males are avid hilltoppers, and it is not unusual to find a dozen or so males on a single summit when conditions are right. Females are less active, spending a good portion of the day resting in between taking nectar and searching for native mustards on which to lay their eggs. Desert Marbles tend to occupy high desert and mid-elevation habitats, usually between 1,500 and 6,000 feet.

Sara Orangetip *(Anthocharis sara)*

FAMILY: Pieridae (Whites and Sulphurs)
RANGE: CA to NM (also western U.S.)
ADULT FLIGHT SEASON: early spring
    (sometimes also late spring)
HOSTPLANT: rock cress, twist flower, and
    other native and exotic mustards
WINGSPAN: 1¼–1⅝ inches

Male

Named for the reddish-to-orange patches on the tips of the forewings, orangetips add a warm splash of color to any spring landscape. Males are most often found along canyon bottoms, rocky hillsides, or steep canyon walls, searching for females. As with the Spring White (see page 18), the presence of Sara Orangetips seems closely tied to colonies of rock cress, although females will deposit their eggs on other mustards as well. While most adults are white, yellow females are not uncommon and, rarely, one may encounter a yellow male. The main flight (when adults are "on the wing") occurs in early spring, but there may be a smaller second brood in some areas, especially following wet winters. Second-brood adults are larger and more lightly marked underneath. Found mainly in high desert, although some populations range upwards into the mountains.

Female

Desert Orangetip *(Anthocharis cethura)*

FAMILY: Pieridae (Whites and Sulphurs)
RANGE: CA to extreme west TX (also NV)
ADULT FLIGHT SEASON: spring
HOSTPLANT: twist flower, tansy mustard, and other exotic and native mustards
WINGSPAN: 1⅛–1⅜ inches

A spring without wildflowers is usually a spring without the Desert Orangetip. These attractive creatures are at the whims of late fall and early winter rains, responsible for germinating the annual mustards that are critical for their survival. Desert Orangetips are more tolerant of dry environs than Sara Orangetips (see previous entry), sometimes inhabiting arid desert flats and mesas. In this variable species, white forms predominate in western areas, transitioning to yellow forms to the east. Females in western desert areas sometimes lack orange on the forewing tip. Males readily hilltop to find females where they, along with other hilltoppers, transform many a Southwest summit into butterfly singles bars. Most populations occur below 4,500 feet.

Orange Sulphur *(Colias eurytheme)*

FAMILY: Pieridae (Whites and Sulphurs)
RANGE: CA to TX (also most of U.S.)
ADULT FLIGHT SEASON: nearly year-round
HOSTPLANT: legumes, mainly alfalfa and sweet clovers
WINGSPAN: 1¾–2 inches

Although widespread and readily encountered in most habitats, this species especially thrives in fields of alfalfa, where they may occur by the hundreds, creating an aerial symphony of orange, yellow, and white. Unfortunately, these infestations are often deemed harmful enough to crops to require commercial control. Orange Sulphurs, like most sulphurs, rarely perch with their wings open. Thus, their brilliant colors are revealed only in flight. Males are bright orange to yellow with a broad black border on the dorsal surface. Females are bright orange or dusky white. There is a silver spot circled by red centrally located on the hindwing underside that readily separates this species from most other Southwest sulphurs. Found throughout most of the year, early-spring individuals are smaller and less orange. Clouded Sulphurs (*Colias philodice,* not featured in this book) are very similar to Orange Sulphurs but are all yellow on top and tend to be more common eastward. Hybridization is known to occur between these two species, and white females of the two species are essentially identical.

Southern Dogface *(Zerene cesonia)*

FAMILY: Pieridae (Whites and Sulphurs)
RANGE: mainly AZ to TX, rarely CA (also eastward along southern U.S. to FL)
ADULT FLIGHT SEASON: nearly year-round
HOSTPLANT: primarily indigo bush and close relatives
WINGSPAN: 1⅝–2¼ inches

This black and bright yellow species is named for the "dog's head" pattern outlined on the forewing, which can be seen on resting, backlit individuals. Widespread across the Southwest, these butterflies may be found in most habitats for most of the year. Males attend mud, along with other sulphurs. Large influx flights are much less common than those of either the Cloudless or Lyside Sulphurs (see next entry and page 22). Late-fall individuals spend the winter in lowlands and are exceptional, flushed with extra pink along the hindwing edges and veins. Adults may be seen flitting about on warm winter days with other sulphurs.

Cloudless Sulphur *(Phoebis sennae)*

FAMILY: Pieridae (Whites and Sulphurs)
RANGE: CA (uncommon), AZ to TX (also eastward along southern U.S. to FL)
ADULT FLIGHT SEASON: most of the year
HOSTPLANT: senna
WINGSPAN: 1¾–2¼ inches

Male

Approximately three weeks after the onset of the summer monsoon rains, tender new growth and flowers appear on our native senna plants, and a wave of large bright yellow and white butterflies envelops the Southwest. This signifies the start of an annual summer ritual—the massive flight of thousands of Cloudless Sulphurs into our region (particularly Arizona and New Mexico) from Mexico (a journey of up to 200 miles or more). It is then that these strong fliers become common, inhabiting mountain as well as desert habitats, persisting into the fall until the senna plants are no longer palatable to their caterpillars. Like many sulphurs, Cloudless are seasonally variable. Summer influx males are generally unmarked lemon-yellow; females are greenish-white, but later females can be white, yellow, or yellow with an orange hindwing flush. Males may form large puddle parties at mud, often with

Female

other sulphurs. Both sexes readily attend flowers and are among a select few butterflies able to take nectar at blossoms with long tubular corollas. Adults may be seen throughout the year, and sometimes following favorable spring conditions, a spring influx of much smaller scale than that of summer may occur. In 2006 a reverse migration southward of hundreds of individuals was recorded in early fall.

Large Orange Sulphur *(Phoebis agarithe)*
FAMILY: Pieridae (Whites and Sulphurs)
RANGE: AZ to TX (also southern FL)
ADULT FLIGHT SEASON: late summer and fall,
   sometimes spring
HOSTPLANT: feather tree (*Lysiloma watsonii*)
WINGSPAN: 1 ¾–2 ¼ inches

Although closely related to the Cloudless Sulphur, this species is generally rare, owing to the scarcity of suitable hosts in the Southwest. Males are a bright apricot color, while females are apricot, pinkish, or creamy white. Suitable stands of feather tree, the larval host, are common just south of the border in Mexico, but it is only the increased use of this plant as an ornamental in some urban areas that has enabled this butterfly to briefly establish itself in the late summer and fall prior to freezing temperatures. Adults may be embedded in influx flights of Cloudless Sulphurs (see page 21), as was the case in 2006. Sometimes seen as early as April.

Lyside Sulphur *(Kricogonia lyside)*
FAMILY: Pieridae (Whites and Sulphurs)
RANGE: AZ to TX (also southern FL)
ADULT FLIGHT SEASON: mid-summer–Dec.
HOSTPLANT: guayacan
WINGSPAN: 1½–2 inches

This small Mexican resident is generally scarce in our region. However, during the monsoons in midsummer, a few Lysides move into the Southwest from Mexico. Once every few years or so these flights number in the hundreds of thousands, perhaps millions! The reasons behind such a large migration are somewhat of a mystery, since except for a few ornamental plantings, there are no known natural hosts for hundreds of miles. Reverse movements from our region south into Mexico have also been noted. Lysides are smaller than Cloudless Sulphurs (see page 21) and are a paler white or yellow with more pointed forewing tips. Most adults have been observed from July through December. In extreme southwestern Texas it is resident, as is its hostplant.

Mexican Yellow *(Eurema mexicana)*

FAMILY: Pieridae (Whites and Sulphurs)
RANGE: AZ to TX
ADULT FLIGHT SEASON: year-round
HOSTPLANT: white-ball acacia
WINGSPAN: 1⅜–1¾ inches

A common pale-yellow butterfly found throughout most of the region, the Mexican Yellow is present all year but is especially abundant following summer rains, when they may be observed in most habitats. Males are attracted to mud, and some puddle parties may number in the dozens. Some individuals move to as far as central California, northern Nevada, and Wyoming, or well up into the mountains, miles from their hostplants. Mexican Yellows differ from most other sulphurs by their pointed hindwing. Both sexes are pale yellow on the dorsal surface and undersides of the wings. Males have a bright yellow streak on the forewing that is barely visible while they are in flight. The hindwings of late fall specimens are more tan underneath, and they seek brown leaves under which they will spend the winter. Winters are spent in low elevations, where a warm, sunny day will coax isolated individuals out of hiding.

Sleepy Orange *(Abaeis nicippe)*

FAMILY: Pieridae (Whites and Sulphurs)
RANGE: CA to TX (also eastward along southern states to East Coast)
ADULT FLIGHT SEASON: year-round
HOSTPLANT: senna
WINGSPAN: 1⅜–1¾ inches

Common but not really "sleepy," these fast, low-flying, apricot-colored butterflies are found throughout the region. It is possible to encounter a Sleepy Orange on any warm day of the year. Although most at home in the desert, adults range far up into the mountains well above colonies of senna, their larval host. Males and females are similar. Late fall individuals are much tanner underneath. The Sleepy Orange is named for the small dorsal forewing dash that resembles a sleeping eye.

Tailed Orange *(Pyristia proterpia)*

FAMILY: Pieridae (Whites and Sulphurs)
RANGE: south-central AZ to western NM
    (also south TX)
ADULT FLIGHT SEASON: July–Dec.
HOSTPLANT: sensitive partridge pea
WINGSPAN: 1¼–2 inches

This summer immigrant from Mexico seeps into our region almost unnoticed following the onset of the summer rainy season. After some weeks, if breeding conditions are favorable, Tailed Oranges multiply to staggering numbers, feeding at flowers and puddling at monsoon-fed creeks and muddy flats. One of the most remarkable sights of late summer is small clouds of male Tailed Oranges taking flight upon being disturbed from their silent salt gatherings—essentially puddle parties gone wild. Summer individuals are bright orange on the dorsal surface and unmarked golden-orange underneath, with a hint of a tail on the hindwing. The hindwings of fall specimens are sharply pointed with brown lines and blotches underneath, a perfect match for the dead leaves under which they'll roost into winter.

Dainty Sulphur *(Nathalis iole)*

FAMILY: Pieridae (Whites and Sulphurs)
RANGE: CA to TX (also eastward along
    southern U.S. to FL)
ADULT FLIGHT SEASON: year-round
HOSTPLANT: dogweed, bur marigold, and
    other sunflowers
WINGSPAN: ⅞–1 inch

Easily overlooked, this tiny yellow butterfly is often found fluttering close to the ground across grasslands, traversing small hills, patrolling canyon bottoms, or flitting about the garden. When first encountered, they might give the impression of a fragile, nondescript butterfly, but Dainty Sulphurs are able to breed far from their Southwest origins, thanks to the polyphagous nature of their caterpillars. However, freezing temperatures in late fall and winter limit them, and winters must be spent in milder climes. On the wing throughout the year, late-season individuals have darker undersides, allowing them to capture the warmth of the winter's sun when their wings are closed.

GOSSAMER WINGS (FAMILY LYCAENIDAE)

The gossamer wings are among our smallest (½ inch to 1½ inches in wingspan) butter-flies. Hairstreaks, coppers, and blues—known for their brilliant colors and delicate patterns—make up this family.

Hairstreaks are named for the tiny tail-like projections on the hindwings of most (though not all) of the species in this family. Many combine these tails with one or more eyespots to resemble a false head. They often slowly rub their hindwings together, drawing attention away from the real head and giving them a fifty-fifty chance of avoiding predation. Most hairstreaks have a rapid, erratic flight, are quick to land, and rest with wings closed.

Blues are renowned for their beautiful hues of blue and purple. Many have beauti-ful, spotted ventral patterns, usually consisting of one or more tiny eyespots on the hindwing. Their flight is erratic but generally not as rapid as that of the hairstreaks. Slow to land, blues will often spread their wings while perched or vigorously rub their hindwings together.

Gossamer-wing caterpillars have a slug-like appearance, and the caterpillars of most blues and some hairstreaks are tended by ants. The ants massage the caterpillars and receive a sugary solution from special glands located on the caterpillars' abdominal segments. In turn, the caterpillars get some protection against potential parasites.

Hairstreaks diapause either as chrysalids or eggs. Blues diapause as either larvae or chrysalids.

Colorado Hairstreak *(Hypaurotis crysalus)*
FAMILY: Lycaenidae (Gossamer Wings)
RANGE: AZ to NM (also CO, UT, south to
 northern Mexico)
ADULT FLIGHT SEASON: midsummer to fall
HOSTPLANT: Gambel oak, silver-leaf oak
 along the border
WINGSPAN: 1¼–1⅜ inches

Fortunate is the observer who catches one of these beauties basking with wings spread, revealing a stunning upper surface that is more reminiscent of a tropical species. Oddly enough, Colorado Hairstreaks are actually more closely allied to hairstreaks found in the Old World. Because of a very short proboscis, they ignore flowers and rarely visit mud, preferring instead to spend most of their time perched on Gambel oak and other trees. Colorado Hairstreaks are especially active on overcast days or at dusk, when adults may be observed darting in and out of oak thickets or dancing about the treetops. Females carefully lay their eggs in bark crevices, where they diapause, hatching with the first tender buds of spring. In most of the species' range, adults fly in midsummer, and in the Southwest, adults persist into the fall—suggesting two broods. Rarely found below 5,500 feet.

Great Blue Hairstreak *(Atlides halesus)*

FAMILY: Lycaenidae (Gossamer Wings)
RANGE: CA to TX (also along southern states
    to FL)
ADULT FLIGHT SEASON: spring to fall
HOSTPLANT: mistletoes on oak, juniper,
    riparian trees, mesquites, and acacias
WINGSPAN: 1¼–1½ inches

    This large tropical species is easily the most brilliantly marked of all Southwest butterflies, with its shimmering turquoise blue upper side. Widespread across the region, adults are relatively common but rarely observed, since they tend to linger in the canopy where their hostplant mistletoes thrive. Fortunately, they are attracted to mud and to small flowers, where they are often approachable. Males can be easily located on strategic hilltops, sitting on the highest point (usually a tree) awaiting females from mid to late afternoon. The underside, festively adorned with sparkling metallic spots of red and black, signifies a warning to predators of distastefulness, a condition resulting from the ingestion of mistletoe by the caterpillars. Spends the winter as a pupa in bark crevices or underneath leaves at the base of mistletoe-infested trees. Also known as the Great Purple Hairstreak.

Desert Sheridan's Hairstreak *(Callophrys sheridani)*

FAMILY: Lycaenidae (Gossamer Wings)
RANGE: southeast CA to northwest AZ and
    southwest UT
ADULT FLIGHT SEASON: early spring, sometimes later
HOSTPLANT: Heermann's buckwheat and other
    buckwheats
WINGSPAN: ¾–1 inch

This spunky little green hairstreak finds its niche in arid limestone canyons of eastern California and northwestern Arizona. Pursuing Desert Sheridans is worthwhile if only just to experience the wild and untamed country they inhabit. Males are feisty, vigorously defending small territories in canyon bottoms against potential rivals while awaiting prospective mates. Females are rarely seen, as they secretly investigate steep rocky slopes in search of their buckwheat hosts. Found mainly in early spring, although favorable conditions can lead to later broods as well.

Juniper Hairstreak *(Callophrys gryneus)*

FAMILY: Lycaenidae (Gossamer Wings)
RANGE: CA to TX (and most of the U.S.)
ADULT FLIGHT SEASON: spring to fall
HOSTPLANT: alligator bark juniper, California
   juniper, one-seed juniper, and relatives
WINGSPAN: ¾–1 inch

Whether visiting flowers or taking salt from mud, this hairstreak is a stunning example of nature's camouflage. With a rich blend of green and brown, punctuated by white lines and dashes, Juniper Hairstreaks are especially cryptic while roosting on their hostplant junipers. Equally cryptic are their caterpillars, small slug-like creatures that blend perfectly with the foliage on which they feed. Adults first appear in spring and are on the wing into the fall. Juniper Hairstreak is quite variable across its range, and the Southwest is home to two subspecies. One is widespread, while the other inhabits the desert's extreme western edge in California. Some experts consider these two distinct species.

Xami Hairstreak *(Callophrys xami)*

FAMILY: Lycaenidae (Gossamer Wings)
RANGE: AZ to TX
ADULT FLIGHT SEASON: nearly year-round
HOSTPLANT: sedums, graptopetalum, and
   related plants
WINGSPAN: ¾–1 inch

Perhaps no other resident Southwest butterfly is as secretive as this species. Found only near colonies of the hostplant, it is never common, and its appearance is very unpredictable. Its succulent hostplants are equally rare and are generally confined to steep, rocky canyon slopes. Males set up small territories in canyon bottoms to await females. Females are rarely encountered, and little is known about their behavior. Xami differs from the similar Juniper Hairstreak (see previous entry) by having the white stripe on the hindwing undersides form a crisp "W". Adults have been found in practically all months. Xamis are among the few butterfly species whose caterpillars bore into the leaves of the host.

Sandia Hairstreak *(Callophrys mcfarlandi)*

FAMILY: Lycaenidae (Gossamer Wings)
RANGE: central NM to west TX
ADULT FLIGHT SEASON: spring to early summer
HOSTPLANT: Texas bear grass
WINGSPAN: 1–1¼ inches

Wherever one finds Texas bear grass, one may be fortunate enough to encounter this rarity, found from spring to early summer. Their abundance in any given year appears to be closely tied to the successful blooming of the host shrub. Both sexes can be found in and around stands of the host, either resting on the leaves or attending the flowers. The caterpillars likewise eat the flowers and are tended by ants. Sandia Hairstreaks are primarily found in discrete colonies east of the Rio Grande, but a very accessible locality occurs just southeast of Deming, New Mexico.

Brown Elfin *(Callophrys augustinus)*

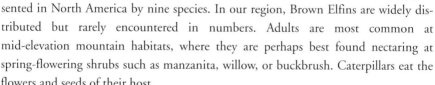

FAMILY: Lycaenidae (Gossamer Wings)
RANGE: AZ (also sporadic across U.S. and
    Canada)
ADULT FLIGHT SEASON: spring
HOSTPLANT: manzanita, many other plants
WINGSPAN: ¾–1 inch

Elfins are primarily a tailless group of spring-flying brownish hairstreaks represented in North America by nine species. In our region, Brown Elfins are widely distributed but rarely encountered in numbers. Adults are most common at mid-elevation mountain habitats, where they are perhaps best found nectaring at spring-flowering shrubs such as manzanita, willow, or buckbrush. Caterpillars eat the flowers and seeds of their host.

Ilavia Hairstreak *(Satyrium ilavia)*

FAMILY: Lycaenidae (Gossamer Wings)
RANGE: AZ to western NM
ADULT FLIGHT SEASON: May–June
HOSTPLANT: desert scrub oak
WINGSPAN: ¾–1 inch

In the somewhat xeric habitat of scrub oaks, this species abounds. Limited in range and generally found off the beaten path, this species is nonetheless fairly common in season—but seldom observed. Both sexes perch on the host tree, remaining still and unseen until disturbed. Males are typically more active than females and can be coerced into flying by lightly tapping the

outer branches of the host. Both sexes are especially fond of the white flowers of yerba santa. Eggs of the Ilavia Hairstreak diapause on stems, hatching with the first buds in spring and enabling the caterpillars to eat the catkins of male plants. Adults fly in May and June in a single brood.

Soapberry Hairstreak *(Phaeostrymon alcestis)*

FAMILY: Lycaenidae (Gossamer Wings)
RANGE: AZ to TX (also OK)
ADULT FLIGHT SEASON: Apr.–June
HOSTPLANT: western soapberry
WINGSPAN: 1–1¼ inches

As the last vestiges of spring fade and the Southwest begins to feel the summer's heat, this silvery-gray butterfly appears, flitting in and about the shaded boughs of western soapberry trees. Soapberry Hairstreaks are closely tied to their host, their life cycle timed to the emergence of the leaves of the tree. Adults utilize other nectar sources in addition to the flowers of the host. Colonies of both tree and bug can be miles apart, and little is known about how colonization occurs. There is one flight annually, between April and June.

Gray Hairstreak *(Strymon melinus)*

FAMILY: Lycaenidae (Gossamer Wings)
RANGE: CA to TX (and most of U.S.)
ADULT FLIGHT SEASON: year-round
HOSTPLANT: flowers and seeds of legumes
    and other plant families
WINGSPAN: ¾–1 inch

Although rarely found in numbers, the Gray Hairstreak is our most familiar and most frequently encountered hairstreak, and the caterpillars of this species are the most polyphagous of our hairstreaks. This versatility allows the adults to occupy just about any habitat, from high mountain meadows to city gardens. The Gray Hairstreak belongs to a large, mostly tropical group known as scrub-hairstreaks. Scrub-hairstreaks, unlike most other hairstreaks, will often bask with their wings open. They are also avid hilltoppers, and male Gray Hairstreaks are often found perched on shrubs or trees on desert summits. Adults can be found throughout the year.

Leda Ministreak *(Ministrymon leda)*

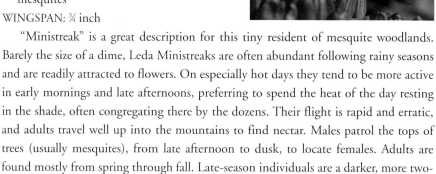

FAMILY: Lycaenidae (Gossamer Wings)
RANGE: CA to TX
ADULT FLIGHT SEASON: spring to fall
HOSTPLANT: velvet, screwbean, and other
 mesquites
WINGSPAN: ¾ inch

"Ministreak" is a great description for this tiny resident of mesquite woodlands. Barely the size of a dime, Leda Ministreaks are often abundant following rainy seasons and are readily attracted to flowers. On especially hot days they tend to be more active in early mornings and late afternoons, preferring to spend the heat of the day resting in the shade, often congregating there by the dozens. Their flight is rapid and erratic, and adults travel well up into the mountains to find nectar. Males patrol the tops of trees (usually mesquites), from late afternoon to dusk, to locate females. Adults are found mostly from spring through fall. Late-season individuals are a darker, more two-toned gray with less red than summer individuals. This tiny hairstreak is distinguishable from all others in the region by its gray-green eyes.

Arizona Hairstreak *(Erora quaderna)*

Female

FAMILY: Lycaenidae (Gossamer Wings)
RANGE: southeast AZ to southwest NM and
 west TX
ADULT FLIGHT SEASON: spring to fall
HOSTPLANT: buckbrush, oak, and probably
 other shrubs
WINGSPAN: ¾–1 inch

This small butterfly, noted for its unusual coloration, is a gem very well worth seeking. Arizona Hairstreaks are avid flower visitors and equally fond of mud, where their congregations, unlike the male-dominated puddle parties of sulphurs, are decidedly coed. At rest, their wings

Male

may be spread, leaving the observer spellbound—particularly by the bright blue irides-cence of the female. Males hilltop, preferring to perch on the twigs and branches of trees or shrubs. Adults are most common in spring but also occur throughout the sum-mer and into the fall.

Marine Blue *(Leptotes marina)*

FAMILY: Lycaenidae (Gossamer Wings)
RANGE: CA to TX
ADULT FLIGHT SEASON: nearly year-round
HOSTPLANT: primarily the flowers and buds
　of legumes and leadwort
WINGSPAN: ¾–1 inch

The alternating brown and gray banding should serve to separate this tropical blue from all others. Marine Blues are unable to withstand freezes, but small numbers are generally present most of the year in warm areas. In late spring, acacias and mesquites provide a profusion of flowers, a favorite food for the caterpillars, and multitudes of adults often appear, dispersing over a wider range than normal, including high up in the mountains. Males are an iridescent purplish brown on top, while females are brown with powder blue centers. Males are strongly attracted to mud, forming puddle parties, which can be large and impressive. Their flight is fairly fast and erratic, more like a hairstreak than other blues.

Western Pygmy Blue *(Brephidium exilis)*

FAMILY: Lycaenidae (Gossamer Wings)
RANGE: CA to TX
ADULT FLIGHT SEASON: nearly year-round
HOSTPLANT: saltbush, Russian thistle
WINGSPAN: ½–⅝ inch

It is said good things come in small packages, and this is certainly true for this desert waif. The smallest of all western butterflies, with a wingspan of less than ½ inch, it is also one of the most attractive—but least noticed because of its size. Pygmy blues inhabit salt flats, roadsides, and marsh edges, especially areas infested with non-native weeds such as Russian thistle, where they often swarm around the shrubs. Their flight is very weak and usually close to the ground, but some-how a few adults venture far to the north or upwards into the mountains away from their normal haunts. Flies most of the year, with colder months spent in warm refuges at low elevations.

Eastern Tailed-Blue *(Cupido comyntas)*

FAMILY: Lycaenidae (Gossamer Wings)
RANGE: southeast AZ to west TX (most of
    eastern U.S., sporadic westward)
ADULT FLIGHT SEASON: Mar.–Oct.
HOSTPLANT: sweet clovers, other legumes
WINGSPAN: ¾ inch

With a small tail on each hindwing, this species may be mistaken for a hairstreak. However, structurally and behaviorally it is a blue. Eastern Tailed-Blues are a common, widespread butterfly across most of North America. In the Southwest they tend to be fairly scarce and somewhat localized. Some suspect our Southwest populations may be of a more recent vintage, following the introduction of weedy clovers caused by the extensive land alteration of the past century. Adults fly from March to October but seem to be most reliable at middle elevations in April and May.

Western Azure *(Celastrina echo)*

FAMILY: Lycaenidae (Gossamer Wings)
RANGE: central AZ to TX (most of western
    U.S.)
ADULT FLIGHT SEASON: year-round
HOSTPLANT: buckbrush, buckthorn, fairy
    duster, and others
WINGSPAN: ¾–1 inch

Although fairly drab underneath, the sky-blue upper side of the male Western Azure is stunning! Females are equally attractive, if not more so, with a violet iridescence enclosed by charcoal black. Although first discovered and named over one hundred years ago, this species is still in taxonomic limbo as scientists sort out the many forms, both regional and elevational, that exist throughout its range. Azures in our region occur from high desert upwards, reaching the tops of our highest peaks. The adults' flight season starts as early as January in lower elevations, with higher-elevation populations emerging later. Males are strongly attracted to mud, usually resting with their wings closed. Formerly known as Spring Azure, which is now considered a separate species.

Sonora Blue *(Philotes sonorensis)*

FAMILY: Lycaenidae (Gossamer Wings)
RANGE: CA (also to northern Baja, Mexico)
ADULT FLIGHT SEASON: early spring

HOSTPLANT: stonecrop
WINGSPAN: ⅝ –¾ inch

Where the Colorado Desert meets the mountains of southern California, one finds isolated pockets of this sparkling little blue. Though not a desert species, Sonora Blues lend their unparalleled beauty to the bleak arid canyons in and around Anza-Borrego Desert State Park (California). One of the first butter-flies of spring, it can be found slowly fluttering over rocky slopes, in gullies, and at the base of cliffs, never far from its host. Both males and females will bask with their wings spread, revealing an upper side of orange-red patches on bright neon blue.

Rita Blue *(Euphilotes rita)*
FAMILY: Lycaenidae (Gossamer Wings)
RANGE: southeast AZ to southwest NM (also
   north to CO, WY)
ADULT FLIGHT SEASON: Aug.–Sept.
HOSTPLANT: Wright's buckwheat
WINGSPAN: ⅝–¾ inch

Male

It is only at the end of the summer rainy season that this butterfly makes an appearance. Rita Blues belong to a large western complex of what are known as buckwheat blues. These small butterflies are very sedentary, for the flowers of the hostplant not only nourish the adults but are required food for the caterpillars. Rita Blues are sexually dimorphic, the male being blue on the dorsal surface, whereas the female is brown. Both are grayish-white under-neath, with black spots and an orange submarginal band on the hindwing. Populations are found at middle elevations, always in colonies of Wright's buckwheat.

Female

Ceraunus Blue *(Hemiargus ceraunus)*
FAMILY: Lycaenidae (Gossamer Wings)
RANGE: CA to TX (also eastward to FL)
ADULT FLIGHT SEASON: year-round
HOSTPLANT: mimosa, lima beans, and other legumes
WINGSPAN: ⅝–¾ inch

Adaptability in butterflies is related to their ability to utilize different hostplants in a variety of habitats. This widespread tropical blue is a good example of this ability. Found throughout the Tropics and on the Caribbean islands, Ceraunus Blues are equally at home in desert canyons and foothills, weedy roadsides, and gardens. Adults avidly visit flowers, and males are often found at mud with other blues. Like Reakirt's Blue (see next entry), Ceraunus caterpillars eat the flowers and buds of many plants in the pea family, but in a given locality the two rarely share the same host.

Reakirt's Blue *(Echinargus isola)*

FAMILY: Lycaenidae (Gossamer Wings)
RANGE: CA to TX (also southern Great Plains)
ADULT FLIGHT SEASON: year-round
HOSTPLANT: indigo bush, white thorn acacia,
  and other legumes
WINGSPAN: ¾ inch

Common and widespread in the Southwest, this species especially thrives in grassland and mountain habitats in summer and fall, with the profusion of blooming legumes. Males often mix with both Ceraunus (see previous entry) and Marine Blues (see page 31) at puddle parties. Under favorable climatic conditions, adults occasionally establish ephemeral colonies far from their normal haunts. In winter, females are able to breed in lowland areas; thus, adults fly year-round. The large curved row of black spots under the forewing serves to distinguish this species from the Ceraunus Blue.

Acmon Blue *(Plebejus acmon)*

FAMILY: Lycaenidae (Gossamer Wings)
RANGE: CA to TX, absent in low deserts (also most of
  western U.S.)
ADULT FLIGHT SEASON: year-round
HOSTPLANT: buckwheats and legumes
WINGSPAN: ¾ inch

Acmon Blues are found throughout the year in the Southwest but tend to be of sporadic occurrence during colder months. Males visit mud, and both sexes attend flowers. Acmon Blues occur from mountains to high deserts. The orange submarginal band visible on both the top and underside of the hind-wing distinguish this blue from most other blues, except Buckwheat Blues (see Rita Blue, page 33), which have little or no trace of orange on the hindwing top surface.

METALMARKS (FAMILY RIODINIDAE)

Metalmarks are a large (about 1,000 species), mostly tropical family of small butter-flies (½ to 1½ inches in wingspan), represented in the Southwest by ten or so species. Only a few of these species have the metallic spots and dashes for which the family is named. Males have reduced forelegs not used in walking. Most have gray, hazel, or green eyes that readily identify them as metalmarks, as opposed to the black eyes found on most hairstreaks and blues. The caterpillars are somewhat slug-shaped and covered with long hairs. Metalmarks diapause as caterpillars.

Fatal Metalmark *(Calephelis nemesis)*
FAMILY: Riodinidae (Metalmarks)
RANGE: CA to TX
ADULT FLIGHT SEASON: year-round
HOSTPLANT: seep willow, virgin's bower
WINGSPAN: ¾ inch

Common and widespread in the Southwest, Fatal Metalmarks largely go about their business unnoticed. These tiny gems belong to a large tropical group of metal-marks known as scintillants. Variable even within a population, scintillants can be dif-ficult to identify with certainty where two or more species co-occur. Regardless, with bright metallic blue flecks adorning both wing surfaces, Fatal Metalmarks are defi-nitely worth a close encounter. Adults usually rest with their wings open but can be secretive, often preferring to perch under leaves. Fatals are found all year, primarily adjacent to creeks and other wet areas, and also in urban gardens.

Arizona Metalmark *(Calephelis arizonensis)*
FAMILY: Riodinidae (Metalmarks)
RANGE: southeast AZ, southwest NM
ADULT FLIGHT SEASON: year-round
HOSTPLANT: bur marigolds
WINGSPAN: ¾ inch

In the narrow, flood-prone gullies and canyons of the Southwest, this tiny bug lives precariously on the edge, for here its entire life cycle takes place. Yet, somehow Arizona Metalmarks persist, defying the whims of nature's fury. Adults behave similarly to Fatal

Metalmarks (see previous entry), and though Arizona Metalmarks are more restricted in range, the two species often fly together and are easily confused. Arizona Metalmarks tend to have a redder background color on the dorsal surface and are less likely to have a darker brown band crossing the upper side of the forewing. Both sexes of the Arizona Metalmark visit flowers, and males can be found close to the ground, usually near the host, especially during the heat of the afternoon.

Wright's Metalmark *(Calephelis wrighti)*

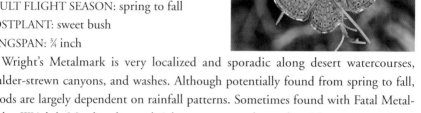

FAMILY: Riodinidae (Metalmarks)
RANGE: CA to central AZ
ADULT FLIGHT SEASON: spring to fall
HOSTPLANT: sweet bush
WINGSPAN: ¾ inch

Wright's Metalmark is very localized and sporadic along desert watercourses, boulder-strewn canyons, and washes. Although potentially found from spring to fall, broods are largely dependent on rainfall patterns. Sometimes found with Fatal Metalmarks, Wright's Metalmarks are brighter orange underneath, with more prominent white wing fringes. Caterpillars of this species gnaw on the stems of the host—a rather unusual behavior for a butterfly.

Zela Metalmark *(Emesis zela)*

FAMILY: Riodinidae (Metalmarks)
RANGE: AZ to southwest NM
ADULT FLIGHT SEASON: early spring and summer
HOSTPLANT: unknown, oaks are suspected
WINGSPAN: 1–1⅜ inches

In the Southwest, where moist canyons laden with sycamores wind through oak woodlands, one may happen upon this small, tan metalmark. Usually found with its wings open, a Zela Metalmark could easily be mistaken for a moth at first, but its clubbed antennae indicate otherwise. Both sexes are best located at flowers, especially yellow or white varieties. Males will sip mud, where they often sit with wings closed. Although the Zela Metalmark is commonly observed, its life history is still not completely known, and its natural hostplant is still to be ascertained. Flies in early spring and again in summer.

Ares Metalmark *(Emesis ares)*

FAMILY: Riodinidae (Metalmarks)
RANGE: southeast AZ to southwest NM

ADULT FLIGHT SEASON: summer and early fall
HOSTPLANT: Emory oak
WINGSPAN: 1–1⅜ inches

Though nearly identical to—and sometimes found with—the Zela Metalmark (see previous entry), the Ares Metalmark is biologically distinct. Ares Metalmarks are more tolerant of drier oak woodland habitats and fly only in summer and early fall. Both sexes visit flowers, especially yellow composites and seep willow. Puddling males usually rest with wings closed, whereby their cryptic undersides render them invisible. The caterpillars diapause, partially grown, in a nest of leaves on the hostplant and take up to nine months to fully develop.

Mormon Metalmark *(Apodemia mormo)*
FAMILY: Riodinidae (Metalmarks)
RANGE: CA to TX (also most of western U.S.)
ADULT FLIGHT SEASON: spring to fall
HOSTPLANT: buckwheats and range ratany
WINGSPAN: ¾–1⅜ inches

This brightly marked species occupies many habitats across the Southwest, with considerable variation geographically. Although they were traditionally treated as a single entity, recent studies indicate our populations probably consist of two or more species. Mormon Metalmarks spend sunny days flitting wildly around patches of buckwheats, often stopping to perch on shrubs or flowers. While sitting, they constantly open and close their wings, revealing a stunning array of colors both on top and underneath. Most colonies in our region are found near stands of Wright's buckwheat. Adults are found from spring to fall, although some populations have only one flight per year.

Palmer's Metalmark *(Apodemia palmeri)*
FAMILY: Riodinidae (Metalmarks)
RANGE: CA to TX (also southern NV)
ADULT FLIGHT SEASON: late spring to fall
HOSTPLANT: mesquites
WINGSPAN: ¾–1 inch

This tiny metalmark ranges across the region in various mesquite habitats, thriving in some of the desert's harshest environments. Few sights of late summer are as spectacular as that of hundreds of Palmer's Metalmarks clustering at the blooms of seep willow in desert washes and gullies. As with other metalmarks, their flight is fast and erratic. Adults fly from late spring to fall, being most commonly seen following monsoon rains.

Nais Metalmark *(Apodemia nais)*

FAMILY: Riodinidae (Metalmarks)
RANGE: southeast AZ (also north to CO)
ADULT FLIGHT SEASON: summer
HOSTPLANT: Fendler's buckbrush
WINGSPAN: 1–1¼ inches

This small orange and black butterfly is often mistaken for a small checkerspot or crescent, but the yellow-green eyes reveal it to be a metalmark. Nais Metalmarks are butterflies of mid-elevations and are always found near Fendler's buckbrush. Territorial males perch on the ground near the hostplant to await females, often engaging rival males in wild, aerial dogfights. Both sexes are fond of flowers, where they sit with wings spread. Sporadic in occurrence and quite localized in our region, they are nonetheless worth seeking.

BRUSHFOOTS (FAMILY NYMPHALIDAE)

This plentiful family includes a number of subfamilies (satyrs, milkweed butterflies, emperors, snouts, true brushfoots, and longwings) that have all been considered, at one time or another, families in their own right. Generalized descriptions for this family are difficult, except that they have just four functional legs, the front two legs being reduced to brush-like appendages tucked below the head—hence the term brushfoot. Adult brushfoots range in size from ½ inch to 4 inches in wingspan. Most brushfoots diapause as either caterpillars or adults.

American Snout *(Libytheana carinenta)*

FAMILY: Nymphalidae (Brushfoots)
RANGE: AZ to TX (also eastward through most of U.S.)
ADULT FLIGHT SEASON: year-round, especially late summer
HOSTPLANT: hackberries
WINGSPAN: 1⅜–1⅝ inches

The American Snout belongs to a small group of peculiar-looking butterflies found worldwide. Snout butterflies have exceptionally long palpi that form a beak-like extension or "snout." The function of this snout is not known, but perhaps it's all a masquerade—when perched on twigs or branches, a snout butterfly looks like a dead leaf. American

Snouts are found sparingly throughout the year, but late-summer migratory flights in the Southwest sometimes number in the millions and garner media attention. Adults nectar at a wide variety of flowers. Male puddle parties can number in the hundreds following summer rains. Adults diapause in winter and may be seen on warm winter days. Fossils of snout butterflies have been found in Florissant shales dating back 35 million years.

Gulf Fritillary *(Agraulis vanillae)*

FAMILY: Nymphalidae (Brushfoots)
RANGE: CA to TX (also eastward to FL)
ADULT FLIGHT SEASON: year-round,
    especially in warmer weather
HOSTPLANT: passion vines
WINGSPAN: 2⅜–2⅞ inches

Few Southwest butterflies can match the brilliant colors of this species. The Gulf Fritillary belongs to the longwings, a group of brightly colored tropical butterflies. Longwings are among the longest-lived of adult butterflies (up to six months as actively flying adults) and are found only where passion vines grow. Historically the Gulf Fritillary's range was limited to mid- to low-elevation canyons with hostplants, but the proliferation of passion vines as ornamentals has allowed them to spread into urban areas. Found sparingly all year in warm refuges, numbers increase with the onset of warmer temperatures.

Variegated Fritillary *(Euptoieta claudia)*

FAMILY: Nymphalidae (Brushfoots)
RANGE: AZ to TX, CA, rarely (also UT, CO, and eastward))
ADULT FLIGHT SEASON: year-round
HOSTPLANT: flax, violets, passion vine, and others
WINGSPAN: 1⅜–2 inches

Primarily a grassland species, the Variegated Fritillary also finds its way into mountains, desert foothills, urban gardens, and other areas. Adults have a tendency to wander far from their normal haunts and have been known to reach Canada. Their flight is direct and usually close to the ground. Both sexes visit flowers. Although sometimes found with the Gulf Fritillary (see previous entry), it is easily distinguished by the absence of silver spots underneath.

Arachne Checkerspot *(Poladryas arachne)*
FAMILY: Nymphalidae (Brushfoots)
RANGE: AZ (also north to WY)
ADULT FLIGHT SEASON: late spring through
    late fall
HOSTPLANT: beardtongues
WINGSPAN: 1–1⅜ inches

This attractive checkerspot is generally common and widespread in the mountains of the West. In our region, however, it is primarily limited to localized colonies in mid-elevation grasslands near good stands of the hostplant. Rarely encountered, males are best located on rises or summits of small hills, where they await females. Both sexes visit flowers. Adults fly in late spring and again from August to October if conditions are favorable. The high-elevation summer population of adults found specifically on Mt. Graham (Arizona) is a darker orange with heavier black markings on the dorsal surface. The name Arachne refers to the spider-like underside pattern.

Fulvia Checkerspot *(Chlosyne fulvia)*
FAMILY: Nymphalidae (Brushfoots)
RANGE: AZ to TX (also north to NE)
ADULT FLIGHT SEASON: spring to fall
HOSTPLANT: paintbrushes, bird's beak
WINGSPAN: 1–1⅜ inches

From Arizona eastward, this handsome checkerspot flourishes in sporadic mid-elevation colonies. Richly outfitted in earthy tones of orange, brown, tan, and cream, Fulvia Checkerspots are most frequently found on rocky limestone hills and outcrops ornamented with the crimson bracts of Indian paintbrush. Adults have been reported flying from spring to fall. Males avidly patrol hilltops to seek females.

Theona Checkerspot *(Chlosyne theona)*
FAMILY: Nymphalidae (Brushfoots)
RANGE: AZ to TX
ADULT FLIGHT SEASON: spring to late fall
HOSTPLANT: Indian paintbrushes, silverleaf, and others
WINGSPAN: 1–1⅜ inches

Most mid-elevation habitats with ample Indian paint-brush will have this butterfly. Though often found with Fulvia Checkerspots (see above), Theonas have a much broader tolerance of soil types, habitats, and hostplants and, consequently, have a much broader distribution, ranging southward to the Tropics. Quite variable both regionally and in any given population, Theona Checkerspots in our region are smartly checkered in various shades of orange and cream on top. On the underside, the hindwing of silvery-white, outlined with black veins and dissected by an orange band, is distinctive. Males are easily located on hilltops; both sexes visit flowers. Theonas are found from spring to fall in a series of broods. Once considered a separate species, the rather scarce Chinati Checkerspot of west Texas is now considered a form of Theona Checkerspot. Chinati relies upon colonies of silverleaf as a hostplant.

Black Checkerspot *(Chlosyne cyneas)*

FAMILY: Nymphalidae (Brushfoots)
RANGE: southeast AZ
ADULT FLIGHT SEASON: spring to late fall
HOSTPLANT: Indian paintbrush and other
    figworts
WINGSPAN: 1–1⅜ inches

This dark checkerspot of the western Sierra Madre barely enters our region along the Arizona border. Black Checkerspot is closely related and very similar to the Fulvia Checkerspot (see page 40), but the two species maintain their genetic identities despite some overlap in range. In recent years, numbers have ebbed and few adults have been reported. Males are avid hilltoppers. Females are best located at flowers. Flies from spring to late fall.

Definite Patch *(Chlosyne definita)*

FAMILY: Nymphalidae (Brushfoots)
RANGE: southeast NM to TX
ADULT FLIGHT SEASON: spring to fall
HOSTPLANT: shaggytuft
WINGSPAN: 1–1⅜ inches

In the seldom-visited lechuguilla agave-covered hills of southeastern New Mexico and west Texas, this small orange checkerspot ekes out its existence. As with other checkerspots, adults won't appear unless climatic conditions are favorable; otherwise, they remain as caterpillars. Similar to Theona Checkerspot (see page 40), this species is smaller and has a pale white spot in the middle of the orange band on the hindwing underside. Adults fly spring to fall, depending on rainfall patterns.

Bordered Patch *(Chlosyne lacinia)*

FAMILY: Nymphalidae (Brushfoots)
RANGE: CA to TX
ADULT FLIGHT SEASON: spring to fall
HOSTPLANT: sunflowers, both native and weedy
WINGSPAN: 1–1¾ inches

This beautiful black butterfly is found throughout the Southwest in a variety of habitats. We find a considerable amount of variation in width and color of the dorsal band, making this one of our most variable butterflies. However, the underside markings are fairly constant, and no other resident butterfly should be mistaken for it. Adults can be abundant, especially in summer and early fall. Males hilltop to some degree but are more likely found at flowers or mud. Some puddle parties number in the hundreds. Females selectively choose plants in the sunflower family with large leaves, in order to lay large egg masses. The caterpillars rest and feed gregariously until the adult butterfly stage—evidently a "safety in numbers" survival strategy.

California Patch *(Chlosyne californica)*

FAMILY: Nymphalidae (Brushfoots)
RANGE: CA to central AZ
ADULT FLIGHT SEASON: spring, sometimes
    summer and fall
HOSTPLANT: desert sunflower
WINGSPAN: 1⅛–1⅝ inches

Although similar to the Bordered Patch (see previous entry) in many aspects, the closely related California Patch has a much smaller range and is restricted to desert hills and canyons that offer thriving stands of desert sunflower. Adults have been most reliably found in spring, with subsequent appearances dependent upon favorable climatic conditions. Colonies are best located by seeking hilltopping males, although both sexes readily attend flowers if and when the desert provides them.

Sagebrush Checkerspot *(Chlosyne acastus)*

FAMILY: Nymphalidae (Brushfoots)
RANGE: CA to west TX (also north to central
    Canada)
ADULT FLIGHT SEASON: spring, rarely late
    summer
HOSTPLANT: desert aster
WINGSPAN: 1¼–1½ inches

Throughout most of its range, this butterfly associates with sagebrush habitats of the Great Basin and as far north as Canada. Southwest populations, once considered a different species, prefer desert washes, canyons, and mid-elevation woodlands, sometimes as high as 6,000 feet. Males do not hilltop, preferring instead to patrol wash bottoms and road dips to locate mates. This species generally flies only in spring, closely tied to the fresh springtime appearance of its hostplant. Flights resulting from summer rain are extremely rare, although once in a great while one might encounter a lone individual in the fall. Adults in eastern areas with more vegetation and more rainfall are darker than those from more arid locations to the west.

Variable Checkerspot *(Euphydryas anicia)*

FAMILY: Nymphalidae (Brushfoots)

RANGE: CA to southwest NM (also most of western U.S.)

ADULT FLIGHT SEASON: spring, rarely early fall

HOSTPLANT: beardtongues, Indian paintbrushes, bush penstemon, and others

WINGSPAN: 1 ¼–2 inches

The stunning checkerboard pattern of this lepidopteran deems this species most worthy of its moniker. Variable Checkerspot is nearly as variable across its range as the Bordered Patch (see page 42), and scientists are still debating the complex relationships and taxonomic issues regarding various populations. Our region boasts three different forms, perhaps involving two species. Two forms associate strictly with bush penstemon, the other with a variety of figworts, but none of the forms occur together. Both sexes frequent gullies and canyons, although males will hilltop. Adults are essentially spring fliers; the summer rains rarely manage to elicit subsequent emergences.

Tiny Checkerspot *(Dymasia dymas)*

FAMILY: Nymphalidae (Brushfoots)

RANGE: CA to TX

ADULT FLIGHT SEASON: year-round, especially spring and late summer

HOSTPLANT: chuparosa, tetramerium, tube-tongue

WINGSPAN: ¾–1 inch

Across the region, in mid-elevation habitats where appropriate members of the acanth family form thriving colonies, one finds Tiny Checkerspots. With a weak, fluttery flight, these miniatures would essentially go unnoticed were it not for their ability to proliferate, especially following summer rains. Adults are quite fond of flowers. Males attend mud or otherwise spend their time slowly cruising stands of the hostplant for females. Some specimens have extra black scaling, overlaying most of the orange on the dorsal wings. Found throughout the year, with adult numbers peaking in spring and again in late summer.

Elada Checkerspot *(Texola elada)*

FAMILY: Nymphalidae (Brushfoots)
RANGE: AZ to TX
ADULT FLIGHT SEASON: spring to fall
HOSTPLANT: desert honeysuckle
WINGSPAN: ¾–1 inch

This diminutive butterfly is often confused with the Tiny Checkerspot (see previous entry). The two species are similar in appearance, size, and behavior, and can be found together. Elada Checkerspots, however, tend to be more localized, being closely tied to stands of desert honeysuckle; also, the marginal band on the Elada's hindwing underside is orange, whereas on Tiny Checkerspots it is white. Elada Checkerspots have close relatives just to the south in Mexico, and their relationship to those species is not yet fully understood. Found from spring to fall in more compact broods than the Tiny Checkerspot.

Mylitta Crescent *(Phyciodes mylitta)*

FAMILY: Nymphalidae (Brushfoots)
RANGE: AZ to west TX (also most of western
U.S., but absent from lower deserts)
ADULT FLIGHT SEASON: spring to fall
HOSTPLANT: thistles
WINGSPAN: 1¼–1⅜ inches

Crescents are small, intricately patterned butterflies named for the crescent-shaped mark near the margin of the hindwing underside. Mylitta Crescents are found from mountain meadows and streamsides down to moist mid-elevation canyons. Males are orange with black markings; females are similar but with paler orange bands. Rarely far from colonies of native thistle; males patrol up and down canyon bottoms to find females.

Pearl Crescent *(Phyciodes tharos)*

FAMILY: Nymphalidae (Brushfoots)

RANGE: eastern CA to TX (also eastward to most of
eastern U.S.)

ADULT FLIGHT SEASON: spring to fall

HOSTPLANT: asters

WINGSPAN: 1–1¼ inches

A familiar sight to butterfly watchers in the eastern
United States, Pearl Crescents in the Southwest are limited
to cienegas, watercourses, and other permanent and semi-
permanent wet areas. Despite the scattered nature of their colonies, adults can be common. Pearl Crescents are surprisingly fast and fly just above the ground, seeking either mates or flowers. The hindwing crescent mark is often obscured by brown scales.

Painted Crescent *(Phyciodes picta)*

FAMILY: Nymphalidae (Brushfoots)

RANGE: AZ to TX (also to OK and NE)

ADULT FLIGHT SEASON: spring to fall

HOSTPLANT: asters, bindweed, and others

WINGSPAN: 1–1¼ inches

In habitats shared by two or more crescents, identification is not altogether easy. For the Painted Crescent the creamy yellow, unmarked underside is diagnostic, but crescents are hyperactive creatures, so glimpses of the underside are often next to impossible. Painted Crescents are found near cienegas, along roadsides, and in alfalfa fields and weedy areas. They are fairly quick in flight, so early mornings are best for photographs, when waking adults bask with wings open to catch the morning sun.

Vesta Crescent *(Phyciodes graphica)*

FAMILY: Nymphalidae (Brushfoots)

RANGE: AZ to TX

ADULT FLIGHT SEASON: spring to fall

HOSTPLANT: tube-tongue, dyschoriste,
and others

WINGSPAN: 1–1¼ inches

This small, orange crescent is most common along weedy west Texas roadsides, becoming scarcer westward. As with other crescents, adults fly close to the ground, often taking nectar from flowers; females rarely wander far from dense clumps of tube-tongue. In southeast Arizona, populations undergo a natural ebb and flow, with adults absent for years between appearances. Vesta Crescents lack the pale buff spots found on Painted Crescents (see previous entry). Flights last from spring to fall and can be rain-induced.

Texan Crescent *(Anthanassa texana)*

FAMILY: Nymphalidae (Brushfoots)
RANGE: AZ to TX, strays to CA
ADULT FLIGHT SEASON: year-round,
    mostly spring to fall
HOSTPLANT: twin seed, honeysuckles,
    other acanths
WINGSPAN: 1–1⅜ inches

Despite its name, this blackish crescent is not restricted to Texas. It differs from other Southwest crescents by the indented margin below the forewing tip, a trait indicating a closer relationship to a large group of tropical crescents to the south. Texan Crescents are most reliably found near colonies of twin seed. Males religiously patrol small territories, often in shaded gullies, to find mates. Females are masters of proliferation. Population numbers of Texan Crescents can suddenly explode into the hundreds of thousands, with adults inundating mountains, foothills, and urban gardens. Then they can just as suddenly disappear, retreating in small numbers to hostplant sanctuaries.

Common Buckeye *(Junonia coenia)*

FAMILY: Nymphalidae (Brushfoots)
RANGE: CA to TX (also most of southern
    U.S.)
ADULT FLIGHT SEASON: year-round
HOSTPLANT: monkey flowers, speedwells,
    plantains, and others
WINGSPAN: 1⅜–1¾ inches

It is difficult to ascertain how a predator interprets the stunningly beautiful pattern of a Common Buckeye. Perhaps the eyespots are intended to represent the eyes of a small vertebrate. Otherwise, it is a superb example of nature's beauty. Common Buckeyes turn up just about anywhere in the region in most years, but they avoid areas of drought and are somewhat scarce at high elevations. Males are rather feisty, defending their territories against all intruders in gullies, along linear pathways, and in road bottoms. Adults are difficult to approach except at the most desirable of flowers. Like other subtropical butterflies, Common Buckeyes cannot tolerate freezing temperatures, so winter retreats to warmer climates are a necessity.

Tropical Buckeye (*Junonia evarete*)

FAMILY: Nymphalidae (Brushfoots)
RANGE: AZ to TX
ADULT FLIGHT SEASON: year-round but
   especially in fall
HOSTPLANT: monkey flowers, speedwells,
   plantains, and others
WINGSPAN: 1⅜–2 inches

The relationship of this species to the Common Buckeye (see previous entry) is still debated. Most experts think of the Tropical Buckeye as a widespread tropical species reaching its northern limits in the Southwest. Others consider it and the Common Buckeye as forms of a single species. Complicating things are the presence of intermediate-looking individuals, difficult to assign to either species. Regardless, at times, these beauties are common, particularly following summer rains when creek bottoms, grassland trails, and road dips become strategic hangouts for territorial males. Differs from Common Buckeye by being darker brown overall, with eyespots more nearly equal in size.

Satyr Comma (*Polygonia satyrus*)

FAMILY: Nymphalidae (Brushfoots)
RANGE: AZ, NM (also western U.S.)
ADULT FLIGHT SEASON: year-round
HOSTPLANT: nettles
WINGSPAN: 1⅝–2 inches

Named for the silvery "comma" mark on the hindwing underside, commas are also known as anglewings, alluding to their jagged wing margins. There are a number of comma species throughout North America. In the Southwest, Satyr Commas occur rather sporadically from around 3,500 feet in elevation and upward in moist habitats. At rest, these butterflies are wonderfully camouflaged. When startled, they flash their bright orange topsides, perhaps equally startling their challenger. Flies in spring and again in fall. Adults may spend the winter in lowland riparian areas.

Question Mark (*Polygonia interrogationis*)

FAMILY: Nymphalidae (Brushfoots)
RANGE: southeast AZ to TX (also to eastern U.S.)
ADULT FLIGHT SEASON: summer and fall
HOSTPLANT: hackberries
WINGSPAN: 2¼–2½ inches

Common and familiar in the East, this species reaches its westernmost limits in the Southwest, where it is uncommon. Question Marks are butterflies of woodlands, where, when resting on tree trunks, branches, or leaves, their irregular wing margins and leaf-like undersides render them invisible. Adults prefer sap, fermented fruit, dung, or mud to flowers. This butterfly gets its name from the silvery question

mark centered in the hindwing underside. There are two annual flight seasons for adults. Summer individuals have more black on their dorsal sides than those in fall. The ventral surface may be marked or unmarked in shades of brown bathed in soft purple hues.

Mourning Cloak *(Nymphalis antiopa)*

FAMILY: Nymphalidae (Brushfoots)
RANGE: CA to TX (also most of U.S.)
ADULT FLIGHT SEASON: year-round,
    diapausing in winter
HOSTPLANT: willows, cottonwoods, elms,
    and others
WINGSPAN: 2½–2¾ inches

The rich maroon and yellow pattern of this butterfly is distinctive. Mourning Cloaks occur throughout temperate North America, and in the Southwest they prefer moist habitats but are liable to turn up anywhere except arid desert regions. To locate females, males perch on trees, shrubs, or the ground along linear pathways. Mourning Cloak adults are known to live for up to ten months. Summer-emerging adults fly through fall then diapause during winter, emerging again in spring when mating commences.

Red Admiral *(Vanessa atalanta)*

FAMILY: Nymphalidae (Brushfoots)
RANGE: CA to TX (also most of U.S.)
ADULT FLIGHT SEASON: year-round
HOSTPLANT: pellitories, nettles
WINGSPAN: 1⅝–2 inches

Ranging across North America, the Red Admiral cannot be mistaken for any other butterfly. In summer, they prefer mountain habitats, avoiding the heat of the deserts below. In fall, adults retreat to the lowlands to spend the winter. Breeding primarily takes place in the mountains in summer, but occasionally breeding may occur in the spring at lower elevations when wet winters initiate the emergence of annual pellitories in lower desert canyons. Males often wait until late afternoon or early evening before setting up territories in sunny alcoves or on hilltops. The hindwing underside presents a delightful tapestry of color.

Painted Lady *(Vanessa cardui)*

FAMILY: Nymphalidae (Brushfoots)
RANGE: CA to TX (also most of U.S.)
ADULT FLIGHT SEASON: year-round
HOSTPLANT: thistles, lupines, mallows, and others
WINGSPAN: 1⅜–2 inches

Also known as the Cosmopolitan, this is the most widespread butterfly in the world, occurring on all continents except Antarctica. In some springs, particularly following wet winters, thousands upon thousands of Painted Ladies migrate northward across Southwest deserts, infiltrating the continent from their winter refuges in northern Mexico. These flights are often so massive as to hinder motorists and attract media attention. Contrarily, adults are scarce to absent during periods of drought. The caterpillars of the Painted Lady feast on a wide variety of plants, enabling them to temporarily colonize any number of habitats. Sometimes mistaken for the much larger Monarch by the uninitiated.

West Coast Lady *(Vanessa annabella)*

Family: Nymphalidae (Brushfoots)
Range: CA to NM, strays to TX (also most of western U.S.)
Adult flight season: year-round
Hostplant: mallows
Wingspan: 1½–2 inches

Although similar in appearance to the Painted Lady (see previous entry), the West Coast Lady does not undergo massive unidirectional flights. In fact, departures from winter retreats along the West Coast are rather subtle, moving eastward as the season progresses. Some adults probably spend the winter in low deserts to exploit fresh patches of globe mallow in early spring. They are more reliably found in small numbers carousing in flower-laden mountain meadows in summer. On the dorsal side, the row of non-connected spots centered in blue on the hindwing, along with the orange spot (not white) along the leading edge of the forewing, should separate this butterfly from the Painted Lady.

American Lady *(Vanessa virginiensis)*

FAMILY: Nymphalidae (Brushfoots)
RANGE: CA to TX (also most of U.S.)
ADULT FLIGHT SEASON: year-round
HOSTPLANT: cudweeds, everlastings, and others
WINGSPAN: 1½–2 inches

American Ladies range throughout the Southwest, often in the company of both Painted and West Coast Ladies (see page 49). For inexperienced watchers, ventral views aid in identification: the American Lady possesses two large eyespots on each hindwing, and the other two a smaller series of four or five. Numbers vary from year to year, but the massive flights reported for Painted Ladies are not known to occur with this species. The American Lady's flight is strong and somewhat erratic, propelling it to all parts of desert landscapes and well into the mountains, where colonies of cudweed await egg-laying females. Adults have been reported in all months, suggesting winter residency.

Red-spotted Purple *(Limenitis arthemis)*

FAMILY: Nymphalidae (Brushfoots)
RANGE: AZ to TX (also to most of eastern U.S.)
ADULT FLIGHT SEASON: spring to fall
HOSTPLANT: willows, cottonwood, and cherry
WINGSPAN: 2½–3 inches

Undoubtedly one the Southwest's grandest butterflies, Red-spotted Purples never fail to delight the viewer fortunate enough to see them. The common name is a misnomer, in that the spots are really orange, and the overall color is iridescent blue. Red-spotted Purple may be a Müllerian mimic of the Pipevine Swallowtail; it may also manufacture its own protective chemicals from ingesting the hostplant, much like the closely related Viceroy (see next entry). Red-spotted Purples are bound to watercourses and other moist canyons lined with willows, cottonwoods, or cherry. Territorial males usually choose to perch on trees or tall shrubs along pathways, roads, or creeks, with their heads positioned outward for optimum surveillance. Adults prefer sap and mud to flowers.

Viceroy *(Limenitis archippus)*

FAMILY: Nymphalidae (Brushfoots)
RANGE: AZ to TX (also most of U.S.)
ADULT FLIGHT SEASON: spring to fall
HOSTPLANT: willows
WINGSPAN: 2¼–2¾ inches

The Viceroy is so closely related to the Red-spotted Purple (see previous entry) that hybrids of the two species sometimes occur. However, the Viceroy looks very different because it has evolved to look like the distantly related Queen, a situation known as Müllerian mimicry, where two distasteful species share anti-predation attributes by having a similar appearance. Like the Queen (see page 54), Viceroys contain distasteful substances to ward off predation. Viceroys are dependent upon willow-lined streams, ponds, and cienegas, rendering some populations vulnerable to lowering water tables and riparian habitat alteration. Adults rarely visit flowers, preferring to stay in the canopy. Viceroys can be distinguished from Queens by the white-edged black line crossing the hindwing.

Weidemeyer's Admiral
(Limenitis weidemeyerii)
FAMILY: Nymphalidae (Brushfoots)
RANGE: AZ (also mountains of western U.S.)
ADULT FLIGHT SEASON: summer
HOSTPLANT: quaking aspen
WINGSPAN: 2–2¾ inches

Not many butterflies match the sheer elegance of a Weidemeyer's Admiral as it soars along a mountain stream on a bright, sunny, summer afternoon. Although generally widespread in western mountains, Weidemeyer's in our region are limited to the aspen forests of the Pinaleño and Chiricahua Mountains. Males establish territories along streams, wide paths, and roads, usually perching at eye level or above. Females spend their time in aspen groves, depositing their eggs on the very tips of selected leaves. Young caterpillars diapause in an aspen leaf rolled into a tube and silkened to the branch (in what is known as a *hibernaculum*), from which it will emerge the following year with the first tender buds of spring.

Goatweed Leafwing *(Anaea andria)*
FAMILY: Nymphalidae (Brushfoots)
RANGE: AZ to TX (also to most of eastern U.S.)
ADULT FLIGHT SEASON: spring and fall
HOSTPLANT: crotons
WINGSPAN: 2¼–2½ inches

In flight, Goatweed Leafwings are a flash of orange. At rest with wings closed, their "dead leaf" masquerade is exceptional. Adults are wary and difficult to approach. When disturbed they choose to land on tree trunks or branches in dense thickets or understory for safety. A good concoction of fermented fruit may lure them into the open. Goatweed Leafwings occur sporadically in the Southwest, finding isolated refuges near reliable colonies of croton. Becomes more common to the east.

Arizona Sister *(Adelpha eulalia)*

FAMILY: Nymphalidae (Brushfoots)
RANGE: CA to TX
ADULT FLIGHT SEASON: late spring
   to fall
HOSTPLANT: oaks
WINGSPAN: 2½–2¾ inches

The prominent white bands and orange forewing tips distinguish this large, handsome butterfly from all others. From late spring to fall, Arizona Sisters course through oak-covered foothills, canyons, and mountains, their bright bold markings often grabbing the attention of non-butterfly-watchers. With their powerful flight, they glide through the canopy of oaks and other trees. While both sexes generally ignore flowers, males are frequent around mud and other damp spots. Formerly known as the California Sister (*Adelpha californica*), a now-distinct species that is confined to oak forests along the West Coast.

Empress Leilia *(Asterocampa leilia)*

FAMILY: Nymphalidae (Brushfoots)
RANGE: AZ to TX
ADULT FLIGHT SEASON: spring to late fall
HOSTPLANT: desert (or spiny) hackberry
WINGSPAN: 1½–2 inches

Of the three resident emperors in the Southwest, the Empress Leilia is the most desert-adapted, frequenting washes and canyons populated with desert hackberry. From spring to fall, adults can be located near stands of the hostplant. Plants containing empress caterpillars or pupae are vigorously defended by territorial males, usually found perched on or near the ground, darting out at all potential intruders—especially rival males. Both sexes are adept at finding sap on the trunks of mesquite and acacia, and even in the slender stems of desert broom, where congregations may number in the dozens.

Hackberry Emperor *(Asterocampa celtis)*

FAMILY: Nymphalidae (Brushfoots)
RANGE: AZ to TX (also to eastern U.S.)
ADULT FLIGHT SEASON: late spring to fall
HOSTPLANT: net-leaf hackberry
WINGSPAN: 1½–2 inches

This emperor occurs in many forms across North America. Populations in the Southwest are closely tied to stands of net-leaf hackberry. Adults perch high in trees, the males using strategic branch tips to defend their territories. Both sexes attend sap leaks and rotting fruit, rarely flowers. Distinguished from the Empress Leilia (see previous entry) by the two inner black spots in the forewing cell, which form a solid bar on Empress Leilia.

Tawny Emperor *(Asterocampa clyton)*

FAMILY: Nymphalidae (Brushfoots)
RANGE: AZ to TX (also to eastern U.S.)
ADULT FLIGHT SEASON: late spring to fall
HOSTPLANT: net-leaf hackberry
WINGSPAN: 1⅝–2¼ inches

Locate a canyon with net-leaf hackberry and, in addition to Hackberry Emperors (see previous entry), you might also happen upon the closely related Tawny Emperor. Like the Hackberry Emperor, this butterfly also has other forms to the east. Southwestern individuals tend to be a lighter brown with fewer markings—a response to a more arid, sun-drenched environment. Male Tawny Emperors can be found darting swiftly around the canopy of hackberry trees, vying for the best perch in which to meet females. Both sexes prefer sap, mud, and rotten fruit to flowers. The species is distinguished from other emperors by the absence of black spots on the forewing.

Monarch *(Danaus plexippus)*

FAMILY: Nymphalidae (Brushfoots)
RANGE: CA to TX (also most of U.S.)
ADULT FLIGHT SEASON: year-round, especially late summer and early fall
HOSTPLANT: poison weed, butterfly weed, and other milkweeds
WINGSPAN: 3¼–3¾ inches

The life history and legendary migrations of the Monarch are well known, making it perhaps the most famous butterfly in the world. However, the Monarchs' main migratory pathways mainly bypass the desert Southwest, rendering them a scarce commodity in our region. Despite this, Monarchs can still be observed all year, especially in late summer and early fall, particularly in wetlands and fields blooming with sunflowers and other yellow composites. Whether western Monarchs winter in Mexico or along the Pacific Coast is not yet known, but dedicated researchers and volunteers continue to seek answers. Males can be distinguished from females by the black pouch on the hindwing, which contains pheromones used in mating. Chemicals derived from milkweeds (eaten as caterpillars) render adults poisonous and distasteful to most predators.

Queen *(Danaus gilippus)*

FAMILY: Nymphalidae (Brushfoots)
RANGE: CA to TX (also eastward along southern states to FL)
Adult flight season: year-round
Hostplant: climbing milkweed, antelope horns, and other milkweeds
Wingspan: 2⅜–2⅝ inches

The Queen is the most common milkweed butterfly in the Southwest, being better adapted to arid habitats than the Monarch (see previous entry). This chocolate-brown milkweed butterfly may be encountered anywhere from the lowest deserts to wooded foothill canyons to the highest mountains. Queens are part of a Müllerian mimicry complex with Viceroys (see page 50). Both sexes are fond of flowers, and males are easily attracted to gardens using plants such as mistflowers, which contain an alkaloid used in mating. Not yet documented as having noteworthy Monarch-like migrations, Queens may undergo subtle movements southward to escape the freezes of desert winters.

Red Satyr *(Megisto rubricata)*

Family: Nymphalidae (Brushfoots)
Range: AZ to TX
Adult flight season: late spring to late fall
Hostplant: grasses
Wingspan: 1–1⅜ inches

Satyrs comprise a large subfamily of brushfoots characterized by slow, erratic flight and forewing veins swollen at the base. Most satyrs come in shades of brown, equipped with one or more round eyespots centered with tiny metallic specks. Typical of these is the Red Satyr, named for the dorsal red patches. Red Satyrs occupy southwestern oak grasslands, shaded canyons, and woodlands. Adults typically fly close to the ground and, upon landing, open and close their wings (sometimes repeatedly) to expose a pair of forewing eyespots, perhaps as a defense mechanism. Males make morning forays to hilltops to seek females. Some—but not all—colonies have both spring and fall broods. Red Satyrs seldom bask with their wings spread.

Canyonland Satyr *(Cyllopsis pertepida)*

FAMILY: Nymphalidae (Brushfoots)
RANGE: AZ to TX (also north to UT and CO)
ADULT FLIGHT SEASON: late spring and
   summer
HOSTPLANT: panic grasses
WINGSPAN: 1½–1¾ inches

Widespread but sporadic in the Southwest, Canyonland Satyrs are the northern-most representative of a tropical butterfly group known as "gemmed satyrs." Named for the metallic gem-like gray patches on the undersides of the hindwings, gemmed satyrs lack the eyespots that typically adorn most of their relatives. Canyonland Satyrs inhabit wooded grasslands, rocky canyons, and streamsides, from middle elevations upward. Adults, with their tan undersides, blend well into backgrounds of dried grasses and low-growing shrubs. Their caterpillars are equally cryptic, looking much like the grass blades upon which they feed. Flies in late spring and summer, with per-haps two broods in some regions.

Nabokov's Satyr *(Cyllopsis pyracmon)*

FAMILY: Nymphalidae (Brushfoots)
RANGE: southeast AZ and southwest NM
ADULT FLIGHT SEASON: spring to fall
HOSTPLANT: bull grass, bulb panicum, and
   other grasses
WINGSPAN: 1½–1¾ inches

From a distance, Nabokov's Satyrs in flight are rather unimpressive, as they slowly flutter just over bunch grasses in shaded understories. Up close, perched in a sunny clearing, they mesmerize with their subtle beauty. This species is an uncommon specialty of mid-elevation woodlands along the border. Adults shun flowers, preferring mud and perhaps rotting fruit instead. Can be difficult to distinguish from Canyonland Satyr (see previ-ous entry) when and where the two fly together. The fall brood is infused with more red markings on a darker tan background.

Pine Satyr *(Paramacera allyni)*

FAMILY: Nymphalidae (Brushfoots)
RANGE: southeast AZ
ADULT FLIGHT SEASON: summer
HOSTPLANT: unknown, probably grasses
WINGSPAN: 1½–1¾ inches

This Mexican species reaches its northern limits along the border in the Huachuca and Chiricahua Mountains of Arizona. It inhabits mountain meadows and springs, usually above 6,000 feet. Males establish loosely defined territories in forest openings and along trails to locate females. Females, apparently reluctant to reveal their true hostplant, lay their eggs in moist areas on a variety of surfaces, including dead pine needles and flowering plants.

Red-bordered Satyr *(Gyrocheilus patrobas)*

FAMILY: Nymphalidae (Brushfoots)
RANGE: AZ to southwest NM
ADULT FLIGHT SEASON: fall
HOSTPLANT: bull grass
WINGSPAN: 1¾–2¼ inches

At the end of the summer rains, this large, blackish satyr makes its annual appearance. Red-bordered Satyrs are confined to grassy Southwest woodlands, where they visit flowers and often congregate at mud in numbers. When provoked to fly they are akin to black holes bouncing up and down steep canyon slopes, barely clearing the tops of bunch grasses as they retreat to the safe confines of the forest. Up close, the underside surface reveals a rich band of maroon, violet, and yellow on a velvety blackish-brown hindwing.

SKIPPERS (FAMILY HESPERIIDAE)

Members of this large, worldwide group are often mistaken for moths. Colored mainly in black, brown, and orange, they hardly match the beauty found in other butterfly families (except in the Tropics). Nonetheless, they are interesting creatures and make up about 40 percent of our butterfly fauna. Most skippers can usually be identified as such by their stout bodies, short wings, and large heads, and by the tips of their antennae, which feature a bent extension known as an apiculus. Skippers range in size from about ½ inch to 3 inches in wingspan.

Four subfamilies occur in our region: firetips, skipperlings, spread-wing skippers, and grass skippers, the latter two groups being the most prevalent. Spread-wing skippers usually land with wings open, and their caterpillars feed on flowering plants. Grass skippers are arguably the fastest of all butterflies. They land with wings closed but may bask in the "jet plane" position. Their caterpillars feed on grasses. Most skipper caterpillars live in nests made of the hostplant leaves (where eventually some, but not all, may pupate) to avoid predation. Some pupate in these nests, but others crawl or drop to the ground and pupate in debris in or around the base of the hostplant. Giant-skippers, our largest skippers, have caterpillars that bore into the fleshy leaves and roots of yuccas and agaves. Most skippers, with some exceptions, diapause as partially grown or fully grown caterpillars.

Dull Firetip *(Apyrrothrix araxes)*
FAMILY: Hesperiidae (Skippers)
RANGE: AZ to southwest NM
ADULT FLIGHT SEASON: July–Oct.
HOSTPLANT: Emory and other oaks
WINGSPAN: 1¼–2 inches

Dressed in brown, with large glassy spots and flocked with orange underneath, Dull Firetips are quite distinctive. Among our largest skippers, they are often common in oak woodlands in midsummer. Adults attend mud but are especially fond of flowers, where they normally sit with wings spread. Dull Firetips are "dull" only when compared with their tropical relatives, known for their brilliant colors and red-tipped abdomens. Dull Firetip caterpillars are brilliantly garbed in maroon and gold but stay hidden in nests of leaves on the hostplant.

Silver-spotted Skipper *(Epargyreus clarus)*
FAMILY: Hesperiidae (Skippers)
RANGE: AZ (also most of U.S.)
ADULT FLIGHT SEASON: late spring to summer
HOSTPLANT: New Mexico locust
WINGSPAN: 1⅜–2 inches

The large silvery-white splotch on the hindwing underside readily identifies this flashy skipper. Silver-spotted Skippers are found above 5,000 feet, usually close to stands of New Mexico locust. Males set up perching sites along trails, roads, and in forest clearings. Adults are attracted to both flowers and mud and usually rest with their wings closed. This is one of only a few skippers that diapause as pupae.

Short-tailed Skipper *(Zestusa dorus)*

FAMILY: Hesperiidae (Skippers)
RANGE: AZ to west TX
ADULT FLIGHT SEASON: spring, sometimes
   summer
HOSTPLANT: oaks
WINGSPAN: 1⅜–1½ inches

   The Short-tailed Skipper, with its lobed hindwing and pale yellowish glassy forewing spots, is one of our more unusual looking skippers. This species inhabits oak woodlands above 5,000 feet. Adults rarely attend flowers. Males are most reliably located on mountain summits, where they perch on trees and tall shrubs or at various mud sources below in well-watered canyons. Females are not often encountered. Short-tailed Skippers are mainly butterflies of spring, with second broods being unpredictable and their numbers usually scarce in summer.

Arizona Skipper *(Codatractus arizonensis)*

FAMILY: Hesperiidae (Skippers)
RANGE: AZ to west TX
ADULT FLIGHT SEASON: late spring to
   late summer
HOSTPLANT: kidneywoods
Wingspan: 1⅝–1¾ inches

   Although uncommon, this attractive species is certainly worth pursuing. The Arizona Skipper is restricted to rocky slopes and watercourses below 5,000 feet in isolated colonies along the Mexican border. Territorial males are best located along gully bottoms, roadside slopes, or at cliff bottoms, where they perch at eye level or higher, often returning to the same branch or rock after being disturbed. In flight their glassy forewing spots often reflect blue in bright sunlight. Females are less often encountered.

Dorantes Longtail *(Urbanus dorantes)*

FAMILY: Hesperiidae (Skippers)
RANGE: AZ (also TX and FL)
ADULT FLIGHT SEASON: July–Nov.
HOSTPLANT: legumes
WINGSPAN: 1⅝–1¾ inches

   In midsummer following the onset of the monsoon, small numbers of Dorantes Longtails seep into the Southwest from Mexico. This is one of our more reliable influx species, although numbers fluctuate from year to year. Their presence lasts only a few months, for, being tropical in nature, they are unable to tolerate the freezes of Southwest winters. Adults visit flowers, usually sitting with their wings closed or nearly so. Males also visit mud and may set up territories, especially late in the afternoon. Dorantes is the most frequently encountered of a half-dozen longtail species that may turn up in the Southwest.

Golden-banded Skipper *(Autochton cellus)*

FAMILY: Hesperiidae (Skippers)
RANGE: AZ to western NM
ADULT FLIGHT SEASON: summer
HOSTPLANT: wild beans, butterfly pea, and
    other legumes
WINGSPAN: 1⅜–1⅝ inches

The golden forewing bands facilitate the identification of this skipper, which is distinct enough to be identified in flight. Adults frequent wooded hills and moist canyons graced with an abundance of wild beans and other legumes. Males perch along roads or in wooded openings, usually with their wings spread. Both sexes attend flowers. There is a single brood in summer.

Desert Cloudywing *(Achalarus casica)*

FAMILY: Hesperiidae (Skippers)
RANGE: AZ to NM
ADULT FLIGHT SEASON: Apr.–Sept.
HOSTPLANT: tick treefoils, butterfly pea, and
    other legumes
WINGSPAN: 1⅜–1¾ inches

This is just one of many medium-to-large brown skippers in the Southwest. Familiarity and a keen eye are required to identify them with certainty. Desert Cloudywings inhabit moist canyons and wooded mid-elevation foothills, usually in close proximity to tick treefoils and other woody legumes. Adults have a bold white patch on the hindwing underside, almost always visible on perched individuals. Males search for females by randomly patrolling canyon bottoms or hostplant colonies. Uncommon, but can be found on the wing mainly from April through September.

Northern Cloudywing *(Thorybes pylades)*

FAMILY: Hesperiidae (Skippers)
RANGE: AZ to TX (also most of U.S.)

ADULT FLIGHT SEASON: late spring to Sept.
HOSTPLANT: cologania and other legumes
WINGSPAN: 1 ¼–1 ½ inches

Northern Cloudywings inhabit foothill canyons, woodlands, and streamsides as well as high mountain meadows. This is our most common and widespread medium-sized brown skipper. Both sexes attend flowers, usually with their wings partially or fully spread. Males sip mud and may gather at puddles in large numbers in favorable years. There is a single annual flight, although late-summer records may represent a much smaller second brood. Colorwise, the plain chocolate brown upperside with small whitish spots and brown fringe distinguish this species from similar-sized skippers in the Southwest. Most medium-sized skippers perch with wings closed or nearly so, not wide open.

Acacia Skipper *(Cogia hippalus)*
FAMILY: Hesperiidae (Skippers)
RANGE: AZ to TX
ADULT FLIGHT SEASON: spring to fall
HOSTPLANT: white-ball acacia
WINGSPAN: 1½–1¾ inches

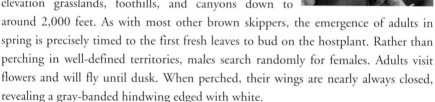

This grayish-brown skipper is widespread across the desert Southwest. The Acacia Skipper occurs in mid-elevation grasslands, foothills, and canyons down to around 2,000 feet. As with most other brown skippers, the emergence of adults in spring is precisely timed to the first fresh leaves to bud on the hostplant. Rather than perching in well-defined territories, males search randomly for females. Adults visit flowers and will fly until dusk. When perched, their wings are nearly always closed, revealing a gray-banded hindwing edged with white.

Gold-costa Skipper *(Cogia caicus)*
FAMILY: Hesperiidae (Skippers)
RANGE: AZ to NM
ADULT FLIGHT SEASON: late spring to fall
HOSTPLANT: white-ball acacia
WINGSPAN: 1¼–1⅜ inches

Closely related to the Acacia Skipper (see previous entry), the Gold-costa Skipper is smaller and less common. Both species use the same hostplant, and their caterpillars may be found together on the same individual plant. Male Gold-costas are highly territorial in canyon bottoms, often skirmishing with various intruders, then returning to the same general perching area. Whether visiting flowers or mud, adults mostly sit with their wings closed. Distinguished from other medium-brown skippers by the gold costa on the forewings.

Golden-headed Scallopwing *(Staphylus ceos)*

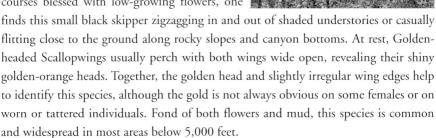

FAMILY: Hesperiidae (Skippers)
RANGE: CA to TX
ADULT FLIGHT SEASON: early spring
  to late fall
HOSTPLANT: goosefoots
WINGSPAN: ⅞–1 inch

In arid desert canyons and along watercourses blessed with low-growing flowers, one finds this small black skipper zigzagging in and out of shaded understories or casually flitting close to the ground along rocky slopes and canyon bottoms. At rest, Golden-headed Scallopwings usually perch with both wings wide open, revealing their shiny golden-orange heads. Together, the golden head and slightly irregular wing edges help to identify this species, although the gold is not always obvious on some females or on worn or tattered individuals. Fond of both flowers and mud, this species is common and widespread in most areas below 5,000 feet.

Arizona Powdered-Skipper
(Systasea zampa)

FAMILY: Hesperiidae (Skippers)
RANGE: CA to TX
ADULT FLIGHT SEASON: year-round
HOSTPLANT: mallows
WINGSPAN: 1–1¼ inches

The soft earthy tones and jagged wing edges allow this skipper to blend with the varied landscapes of the desert Southwest. Looking very much like a brown moth, Arizona Powdered-Skippers are indeed butterflies and not uncommon in rocky canyons and gullies, extending their range upwards to oak woodlands. Males can be found protecting small territories in canyon bottoms or wash junctions. Both sexes visit flowers, where, with wings usually spread, they are easier to spot. Unlike most skipper caterpillars, those of the Arizona Powdered-Skipper continue to feed during winter months; thus, adults are found throughout the year.

Texas Powdered-Skipper
(Systasea pulverulenta)

FAMILY: Hesperiidae (Skippers)
RANGE: AZ and TX
ADULT FLIGHT SEASON: nearly year-round
HOSTPLANT: mallows
WINGSPAN: 1–1¼ inches

Essentially identical to the Arizona Powdered-Skipper (see previous entry) in both looks and behavior, this skipper is more at home in the arid regions of west Texas. Both there and in isolated spots along the Mexican border, the two powdered-skippers mingle, and correctly identifying the two is difficult. On the Texas Powdered-Skipper the pale median band on the forewing has a smoothly curved inner edge. This inner edge is jagged on the Arizona Powdered-Skipper.

Sleepy Duskywing *(Erynnis brizo)*

FAMILY: Hesperiidae (Skippers)
RANGE: AZ to TX (also most of U.S.)
ADULT FLIGHT SEASON: spring
HOSTPLANT: Emory, Arizona, and other oaks
WINGSPAN: 1¼–1½ inches

Duskywings comprise a baffling group of spread-wing skippers represented in the Southwest by ten species. Medium-sized (1 to 1½ inches), with mottled brown forewings, most are so similar that identifying them by species is difficult even for experts. The brown fringe and lack of small white forewing spots distinguishes this species from other duskywings. The Sleepy Duskywing flies only in spring, when it courses through oak woodlands from middle to high elevations. Males use both mountain summits and canyon bottoms to locate mates. Females prefer to lay their eggs on oak seedlings. Whereas most duskywing caterpillars feed for a month, Sleepy Duskywing caterpillars feed for six months before entering diapause in mid-October.

Juvenal's Duskywing *(Erynnis juvenalis)*

FAMILY: Hesperiidae (Skippers)
RANGE: AZ, southwest NM to TX (sporadic in TX; also most of eastern U.S.)
ADULT FLIGHT SEASON: spring through summer
HOSTPLANT: Emory, Arizona, and other oaks
WINGSPAN: 1¼–1½ inches

Sporting a brown fringe across most of its range everywhere else, Juvenal's Dusky-wings in the Southwest have a white fringe, adding it to a confusing array of similar duskywings. Juvenal's are limited to oak woodlands along the Mexican border, where they frequent flowers and damp spots such as mud seeps. Although they are usually somewhat larger than similar species, reliable identification is difficult.

Mournful Duskywing *(Erynnis tristis)*

FAMILY: Hesperiidae (Skippers)
RANGE: CA to TX
ADULT FLIGHT SEASON: early spring to late fall
HOSTPLANT: oaks
WINGSPAN: 1⅜–1½ inches

This duskywing ranges across Southwest oak woodlands. Identifiable by the white submargin along the hindwing undersides, Mournful Duskywings tolerate more arid regions than do their relatives. Their increasing presence in urban areas may be attributable to the growing popularity of non-native oaks as ornamentals. Adults visit both flowers and mud, where they perch with their wings spread. Males hilltop with other duskywings.

Pacuvius Duskywing *(Erynnis pacuvius)*

FAMILY: Hesperiidae (Skippers)
RANGE: AZ to NM (also most of western U.S.)
ADULT FLIGHT SEASON: early spring to fall
HOSTPLANT: Fendler's buckbrush
WINGSPAN: 1¼–1⅜ inches

Slightly smaller than the two previous white-fringed duskywings, Pacuvius Dusky-wings are nonetheless difficult to identify with certainty. The orange-brown patches on the forewings will help to distinguish most freshly emerged (before they lose any of their scales) individuals. Adults avidly visit flowers, often those of their hostplant. Males hilltop or sip from mud. There are two flights—one in spring and again in sum-mer—although records of sightings extend well into fall. If you see females laying their eggs on Fendler's buckbrush, you know they are Pacuvius Duskywings.

Funereal Duskywing *(Erynnis funeralis)*

FAMILY: Hesperiidae (Skippers)
RANGE: CA to TX (also eastward to AR and LA)
ADULT FLIGHT SEASON: year-round
HOSTPLANT: New Mexico locust, baby bon-
    nets, and other legumes, janusia
WINGSPAN: 1½ inches

This versatile species is our most frequently encountered duskywing. Funereal Duskywings range widely across the region from desert foothills to high mountains, utilizing a wide variety of legumes as hostplants for their caterpillars. Compared with other duskywings, the Funereal's forewing is slightly longer and narrower. The pale brown patch at the end of the forewing cell is also a distinguishing characteristic. Males locate females by perching along roads and trails, where they flutter around tirelessly, rarely stopping for rest.

White Checkered-Skipper
(Pyrgus albescens)

FAMILY: Hesperiidae (Skippers)
RANGE: CA to TX (also southern states to FL)
ADULT FLIGHT SEASON: year-round
HOSTPLANT: mallows
WINGSPAN: 1–1¼ inches

Small skippers with dark brown-and-white checkered patterns are obviously checkered-skippers but, like duskywings, their exact species are more difficult to discern. The White Checkered-Skipper is identical to the Common Checkered-Skipper (see next entry), with which it shares range and habitat in part, and cannot be separated from it except by lab dissection. White Checkered-Skippers skirt low to the ground in fields, gardens, and waste places, as well as in grasslands and desert canyons. Adults fly all year and come readily to flowers, where they perch with wings spread.

Common Checkered-Skipper
(Pyrgus communis)

FAMILY: Hesperiidae (Skippers)
RANGE: AZ to TX (also most of U.S.)
ADULT FLIGHT SEASON: spring to fall
HOSTPLANT: mallows
WINGSPAN: 1–1¼ inches

The complement to the White Checkered-Skipper (see previous species, including photo), this species is better adapted to moist, colder habitats found at higher altitudes and farther to the north. The two occur together at times, making reliable identification impossible. Common Checkered-Skippers are almost always present in mountain meadows and forest clearings in summer. Adults "skip" close to the ground in search of nectar or mud. Females have more black than males and are less often encountered.

Desert Checkered-Skipper
(Pyrgus philetas)
FAMILY: Hesperiidae (Skippers)
RANGE: AZ to TX
ADULT FLIGHT SEASON: year-round
HOSTPLANT: mallows
WINGSPAN: ¾–1 inch

This subtropical species barely enters our area along the Mexican border. Often found with the White Checkered-Skipper (see page 64), this species is distinguished by the plain, washed-out underside and by having the checkered white-and-black spots on the forewing margin more evenly spaced. Desert Checkered-Skippers dwell in the bottoms of arid desert canyons, along roadsides, and in other locations with weedy, prostrate mallows, rarely venturing above middle elevations. Males are avid puddlers and may congregate together in numbers. Adults are recorded in all months, suggesting non-diapausing caterpillars.

Erichson's White-Skipper
(Heliopetes domicella)
FAMILY: Hesperiidae (Skippers)
RANGE: AZ to TX
ADULT FLIGHT SEASON: year-round
HOSTPLANT: mallows
WINGSPAN: 1–1¼ inches

White-skippers look like slightly larger versions of checkered-skippers. Erichson's White-Skipper has a broad white band separating a brown base and a checkered outer edge on the dorsal surface of the wings. This skipper is at home in the rocky hills and parched washes of the Southwest. Although they are rarely found in numbers, an afternoon stroll down a saguaro-studded canyon decked with a profusion of mallows should yield a male or two.

Northern White-Skipper
(Heliopetes ericetorum)
FAMILY: Hesperiidae (Skippers)
RANGE: CA to AZ (also most of western U.S.)
ADULT FLIGHT SEASON: late spring and
    early fall
HOSTPLANT: mallows
WINGSPAN: 1¼–1⅜ inches

Female (top), male (below)

Widespread in the West, Northern White-Skippers maintain strong but isolated colonies in the chaparral of remote desert mountains and central Arizona foothills. These fast-flying skippers appear in late spring, just prior to the blistering heat of summer. Both sexes attend flowers, and small puddle parties of males may materialize in favorable habitats. Adults are dimorphic, with the males being mostly white and the females darker near the base of the dorsal wings, with checkered outer forewings. Adults may spread far beyond their normal range but fail to establish residency despite the availability of desert mallows. Adults' flight seasons occur in late spring and again in early fall.

Common Streaky Skipper *(Celotes nessus)*
FAMILY: Hesperiidae (Skippers)
RANGE: AZ to TX
ADULT FLIGHT SEASON: spring and summer
HOSTPLANT: ayenia (a member of the
  chocolate family)
WINGSPAN: ¾–⅞ inch

This delicate, weak-flying little skipper is easily overlooked, owing to its small size, yet when perched with its wings open, it presents a striking pattern of lines, chevrons, and spots. Common Streaky Skippers occupy the bottoms of desert canyons and foothill slopes up to 5,000 feet, where they frequent mud and flowers. It cannot be easily confused with any other skipper except in isolated areas of west Texas, where the nearly identical Scarce Streaky-Skipper (*Celotes limpia*) overlaps its range. Adults fly in spring and again in summer.

Common Sootywing *(Pholisora catullus)*
FAMILY: Hesperiidae (Skippers)
RANGE: CA to TX (also most of U.S.)
ADULT FLIGHT SEASON: Apr.–Oct.
HOSTPLANT: pigweeds
WINGSPAN: ⅞–1 inch

This small, velvety black skipper occurs in a variety of habitats across its range. In the Southwest it prefers weedy areas, especially those infested with pigweed. The term "common" is misapplied regarding this species, for it is uncommon to encounter more than a few individuals on any particular day, although the species may be found anywhere below 6,000 feet. The row (or rows) of tiny white dots on the dorsal side of the forewing vary individually in size and number, but the third dot down from the leading edge or costa is usually noticeably displaced outward. Adults may be seen flying weakly, close to the ground, from April to October.

Mojave Sootywing *(Hesperopsis libya)*

FAMILY: Hesperiidae (Skippers)
RANGE: CA to central AZ (also north to
   MT and ND)
ADULT FLIGHT SEASON: spring to fall
HOSTPLANT: saltbush
WINGSPAN: ¾–1 inch

The phrase "some like it hot" certainly applies to this species. In the arid western deserts where few other butterflies live, one finds Mojave Sootywings flitting about saltbush-laden alkali flats, seemingly oblivious to the desert's heat. Though saltbush covers vast areas, colonies can be localized, probably in relation to reliable sources of nectar. Flights of adult butterflies occur before and after the blistering heat of summer, although the caterpillars somehow survive months of triple-digit temperatures, tucked away in nests of the hostplant. Compared with markings on the Common Sootywing (see previous entry), the third white dot on the Mojave's forewing is only slightly displaced outward.

Saltbush Sootywing *(Hesperopsis alpheus)*

FAMILY: Hesperiidae (Skippers)
RANGE: AZ to TX (also NV and CO)
ADULT FLIGHT SEASON: spring and summer
HOSTPLANT: four-wing saltbush
WINGSPAN: ⅞–1 inch

The mottled brown forewing distinguishes this from other sootywings. Saltbush Sootywings share a portion of their range with Mojave Sootywings (see previous entry), but direct competition seems minimal, and Saltbush Sootywings are more tolerant of cold temperatures, occupying saltbush stands up to 5,000 feet. Adults concentrate in and around hostplant colonies but may wander in search of nectar. Males course over the tops of shrubs, seemingly never stopping to rest in their quest for females.

Four-spotted Skipperling
(Piruna polingii)

FAMILY: Hesperiidae (Skippers)
RANGE: AZ (also sporadic in NM and TX)
ADULT FLIGHT SEASON: summer
HOSTPLANT: grasses
WINGSPAN: ¾–⅞ inch

This tiny skipper has a spotty distribution across its range, found in some mountains but absent from others. In the Huachuca and Chiricahua Mountains, Four-spotted Skipperlings are most numerous along moist, shaded hillsides, streams, and springs. The females lay their eggs on various grasses in these localized habitats, for their caterpillars require high levels of humidity to survive winters. Adults fly weakly, seeking mud or flowers. Perches with both wings spread in unison, a trait it shares with its relatives.

Tropical Least Skipper *(Ancyloxypha arene)*
FAMILY: Hesperiidae (Skippers)
RANGE: AZ to TX
ADULT FLIGHT SEASON: spring to fall
HOSTPLANT: grasses
WINGSPAN: ⅝–⅞ inch

In desert lowlands along the Mexican border, where water is permanent, or nearly so, one may stumble upon Tropical Least Skippers. This tiny orange skipper wends it way slowly through thick grasses along streams and cienegas, seeking nectar or, in the case of the females, oviposition sites. Following summers with abundant rainfall, wandering females utilize temporary wetlands to establish colonies far from their normal haunts. Numbers fluctuate widely from year to year, probably owing to their tropical nature and sensitivity to rainfall patterns.

Edward's Skipperling *(Oarisma edwardsii)*
FAMILY: Hesperiidae (Skippers)
RANGE: AZ to TX (also north to CO)
ADULT FLIGHT SEASON: summer
HOSTPLANT: grasses
WINGSPAN: 1 inch

Although distributed widely across the Southwest, colonies of Edward's Skipperling tend to be localized in wooded uplands of oak and pine. Adults fly weakly close to the ground in thick grassy areas and are rarely common. Both sexes attend flowers. Males appear to randomly seek females rather than define a specific territory. Females lay their eggs on grasses along gully bottoms.

Orange Skipperling *(Copaeodes aurantiaca)*
FAMILY: Hesperiidae (Skippers)
RANGE: CA to TX
ADULT FLIGHT SEASON: year-round

HOSTPLANT: Bermuda grass, side-oats grama, and others

WINGSPAN: ¾–⅞ inch

"Small but fast" best describes this common skipper. Orange Skipperlings stealthily occupy arid desert canyons, mainly below 7,000 feet, where they literally go unnoticed, save by the skilled observer. Males avidly patrol wash bottoms and are so quick in flight that close looks can be had only once they alight on a rock or low twig. Females, when not at flowers, inspect the shaded pockets on hillsides and cliffs for suitable grasses upon which to lay their eggs. Adults also frequent urban gardens. The caterpillar, unlike those of most grass-feeding skippers, makes no nest during its development.

Fiery Skipper *(Hylephila phyleus)*
FAMILY: Hesperiidae (Skippers)
RANGE: CA to TX (also eastward to FL)
ADULT FLIGHT SEASON: year-round
HOSTPLANT: Bermuda and other grasses
WINGSPAN: ⅞–1¼ inches

Male

Wherever Bermuda grass has gained a foothold, this skipper has followed. In towns and cities this skipper can be a common sight zipping about lawns, gardens, golf courses, and parks. In natural habitats, adults tend to be scarce and localized around well-watered weedy areas with non-native grasses. Fiery skippers are easily attracted to yards with lantana and other flowers. The sexes are dimorphic. Males are bright orange with a narrow black stigma on the forewing; females have more black on the dorsal side and are darker-shaded underneath. Their caterpillars construct horizontal nests at the base of grasses, avoiding the cutting blades of lawnmowers.

Female

Pahaska Skipper *(Hesperia pahaska)*
FAMILY: Hesperiidae (Skippers)
RANGE: CA to TX north through Rocky Mountains to Canada)
ADULT FLIGHT SEASON: spring to fall
HOSTPLANT: blue grama grass
WINGSPAN: ⅞–1¼ inches

Among various butterfly groups, there are inevitable identification challenges. The Pahaska and Green (see next entry) Skippers are a case in point. While the prominent chevron of white spots on a yellowish-green hindwing distinguishes the Pahaska Skipper from most others in the Southwest, it certainly does not help

distinguish it from the Green Skipper. Pahaska Skippers occur on grassy wooded hillsides and open grasslands, as well as desert foothills. Males patrol hilltops or high points along ridge lines to seek females. Both sexes come to nectar. Males in jet-plane posture show a large black stigma.

Green Skipper *(Hesperia viridis)*
FAMILY: Hesperiidae (Skippers)
RANGE: AZ to TX (north to WY)
ADULT FLIGHT SEASON: summer in AZ, late
   spring to summer in NM and TX
HOSTPLANT: grasses
WINGSPAN: 1–1⅜ inches

This look-alike to the Pahaska Skipper (see previous entry) is most common in the oak-studded arid canyons and grasslands of New Mexico and west Texas. Unlike the Pahaska Skipper, males use gully bottoms to locate females. Both sexes visit flowers. The ventral (underside) pattern of this species closely resembles Pahaska Skipper's, and the two are not reliably distinguished from one another in areas of overlap, without dissection. In most areas there are two broods.

Sachem *(Atalopedes campestris)*
FAMILY: Hesperiidae (Skippers)
RANGE: CA to TX (also most of southern U.S.)
ADULT FLIGHT SEASON: Apr. to fall
HOSTPLANT: Bermuda and other weedy
   grasses
WINGSPAN: 1–1⅜ inches

Male

Like the Fiery Skipper (see page 69), Sachems have followed invasive grasses into cities and towns. However, they are not nearly as common as Fiery Skippers and seem to be more successful in non-native weedy wetland and agricultural habitats with non-native grasses. Adults wander into mountains on occasion, but attempts to colonize there seem to fail. Males, when perched with wings open, reveal a large squarish stigma. Females have a pale white chevron underneath and are often mistaken for Green, Pahaska, or similar skippers. With wings open, females show a large window-like spot near the cell. Adults occur from April through fall, indicating a mid-elevation residence.

Female

Carus Skipper *(Polites carus)*
FAMILY: Hesperiidae (Skippers)
RANGE: AZ to TX
ADULT FLIGHT SEASON: spring to summer
HOSTPLANT: probably grasses
WINGSPAN: 1–1¼ inches

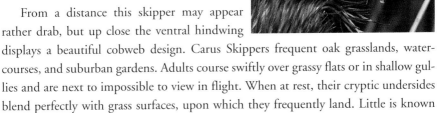

From a distance this skipper may appear rather drab, but up close the ventral hindwing displays a beautiful cobweb design. Carus Skippers frequent oak grasslands, watercourses, and suburban gardens. Adults course swiftly over grassy flats or in shallow gullies and are next to impossible to view in flight. When at rest, their cryptic undersides blend perfectly with grass surfaces, upon which they frequently land. Little is known of their life cycle, but judging from their range and habitat, many grasses probably serve as hosts.

Taxiles Skipper *(Poanes taxiles)*
FAMILY: Hesperiidae (Skippers)
RANGE: AZ to NM (also northward to SD and WY)
ADULT FLIGHT SEASON: June–Sept.
HOSTPLANT: grasses
WINGSPAN: 1–1¼ inches

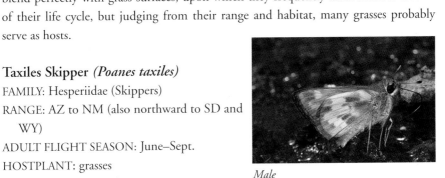

Male

In the sky islands during summer, this is perhaps the most conspicuous orange skipper. Taxiles Skippers are common from mid-elevation wooded areas up to mountain meadows. Males flash bright golden-orange uppersides as they patrol along roads, trails, and forest clearings seeking mates. Females are darker on top, with shades of brown and violet underneath. Both sexes visit thistles, mint, and other mountain flowers. There is one adult flight season per year, lasting from June into September.

Female

White-barred Skipper *(Atrytonopsis pittacus)*

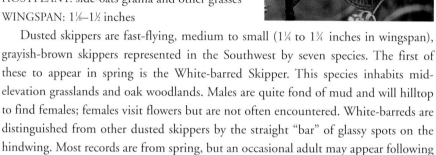

FAMILY: Hesperiidae (Skippers)

RANGE: AZ to TX

ADULT FLIGHT SEASON: spring, occasionally
  after summer rains

HOSTPLANT: side-oats grama and other grasses

WINGSPAN: 1⅛–1½ inches

Dusted skippers are fast-flying, medium to small (1¼ to 1¾ inches in wingspan), grayish-brown skippers represented in the Southwest by seven species. The first of these to appear in spring is the White-barred Skipper. This species inhabits mid-elevation grasslands and oak woodlands. Males are quite fond of mud and will hilltop to find females; females visit flowers but are not often encountered. White-barreds are distinguished from other dusted skippers by the straight "bar" of glassy spots on the hindwing. Most records are from spring, but an occasional adult may appear following summer rains, especially along the Mexican border.

Python Skipper *(Atrytonopsis python)*

FAMILY: Hesperiidae (Skippers)

RANGE: AZ to TX

ADULT FLIGHT SEASON: Apr.–July

HOSTPLANT: probably grass

WINGSPAN: 1¼–1½ inches

Adult Python Skippers emerge during the last days of spring at the onset of the dry season. They frequent grasslands, mixed woodlands, and canyons of middle elevations. Widespread but rarely common, one must usually locate them at thistles, yellow composites, cholla, or other preferred flowers for close looks. Nothing has yet been reported of its early stages. However, it seems the eggs are timed to hatch just prior to the monsoon rains, to allow caterpillars to exploit the oncoming fresh leaves of summer grasses. Python Skippers are distinguished from other dusted skippers by the bold hindwing pattern, with the spot bar curving outward, and by yellowish glassy spots on the forewing. Texas individuals have reduced markings underneath. Records exist from April to July.

Sheep Skipper *(Atrytonopsis edwardsi)*

FAMILY: Hesperiidae (Skippers)

RANGE: AZ and west TX

ADULT FLIGHT SEASON: late spring, late summer

HOSTPLANT: side-oats grama

Wingspan: 1¼–1½ inches

Sheep Skippers occupy mid-elevation canyons and foothills with ample supplies of side-oats grama and other bunch grasses. Among dusted skippers, this species is the most xeric-adapted, with some populations extending down to the desert's edge. Adults streak back and forth along canyon walls, with males predictably choosing strategic rocks or shrubs as lookouts for females. As with all dusted skippers, adults have a long proboscis that allows them to reach nectar in long, tubular flowers. The hindwing underside is powdered gray, with a random and variable array of pale spots. There are two adult flight seasons annually, one in late spring and one in late summer.

Viereck's Skipper *(Atrytonopsis vierecki)*

FAMILY: Hesperiidae (Skippers)
RANGE: eastern AZ to west TX (also north to CO)
ADULT FLIGHT SEASON: Apr.–June
HOSTPLANT: probably grasses
WINGSPAN: 1¼–1½ inches

Viereck's Skipper dwells primarily in the arid oak-juniper woodlands of New Mexico and west Texas. Males patrol gullies, ravines, and arid steep-walled canyons, perching on rocks, high walls, or tall shrubs for maximum advantage in locating females. No details of the Viereck's Skipper's life cycle have been reported, owing perhaps to its remote habitats and uncommon nature. May be found with Python Skipper (see page 72), but the plain underside with two parallel lines should distinguish it.

Bronze Roadside-Skipper
(Amblyscirtes aenus)

FAMILY: Hesperiidae (Skippers)
RANGE: AZ to TX (also sporadic eastward)
ADULT FLIGHT SEASON: spring to summer
HOSTPLANT: grasses
WINGSPAN: 1 inch

Roadside skippers are small brownish skippers, represented in the Southwest by more than a dozen species. Most have similar patterns with only subtle differences, making them a challenge to identify by species. The Bronze Roadside-Skipper is the most frequently encountered and occurs from mid-elevation oak woodlands to lower coniferous forests. Adults are most active in mornings, seeking the shade of canyon walls or trees during the heat of the day. Males patrol along gullies and canyons, using a variety of perching surfaces, often at the base of cliffs or steep slopes. Both sexes attend flowers. Individuals in Arizona are more boldly marked than those found eastward.

Dotted Roadside-Skipper *(Amblyscirtes eos)*

FAMILY: Hesperiidae (Skippers)
RANGE: AZ to TX
ADULT FLIGHT SEASON: spring to fall
HOSTPLANT: obtuse panic-grass (vine mesquite)
WINGSPAN: ⅞–1 inch

The fine, white-dotted ventral side would normally separate this species from others, were it not for three similar species found in its range. Dotted Roadside-Skippers favor lowland oak and grassland habitats with well-established hostplant colonies. When not visiting flowers, adults often perch on the ground, where they are difficult to spot. Males patrol benches along gullies, roadsides, and small creeks to find mates. The absence of a white cell spot on the dorsal forewing and the presence of black outlining the white spots on the hindwing underside will aid in separating this species from others in its sect.

Large Roadside-Skipper
(Amblyscirtes exoteria)

FAMILY: Hesperiidae (Skippers)
RANGE: AZ to extreme western NM
ADULT FLIGHT SEASON: summer
HOSTPLANT: bull grass
WINGSPAN: 1–1¼ inches

This species is "large" only when compared with other roadies. Large Roadside-Skippers occur from oak-juniper woodlands up to mixed pine-oak forests. Adults are most often observed nectaring at thistle or other favored flowers. Freshly emerged Large Roadside-Skippers convey a subtle beauty that can best be appreciated with the aid of close-focusing binoculars. For some reason this species does not completely follow the distribution of its hostplant into the wilds of New Mexico and west Texas. There is one adult flight season in summer.

Nysa Roadside-Skipper *(Amblyscirtes nysa)*

FAMILY: Hesperiidae (Skippers)
RANGE: AZ to TX (also KS and MO)
ADULT FLIGHT SEASON: Mar.–Oct.
HOSTPLANT: grasses
WINGSPAN: ⅞ inch

The mottled black and brown underside distinguishes this small skipper from others. Nysa Roadside-Skippers occur from mid-elevation oak woodlands down to mesquite grasslands. In summer, adults are most active during the first few hours following sunrise. Males perch on the ground in gully bottoms or road depressions to locate females. As with other roadside skippers, adults spend the warmer part of the day at flowers or resting in the shade.

Eufala Skipper *(Lerodea eufala)*
FAMILY: Hesperiidae (Skippers)
RANGE: CA to TX (also to FL along southern states)
ADULT FLIGHT SEASON: year-round
HOSTPLANT: Bermuda, Johnson, and other grasses
WINGSPAN: 1–1⅛ inches

This gray-brown skipper is distinguished by its overall plainness. Much like the Fiery Skipper (see page 69), this species has benefited from the proliferation of invasive grasses and is more liable to be found around human habitation than in natural situations. Scarce early in the year, its numbers increase as the year progresses. Adults are fond of lantana and other ornamental flowers. Upon landing, adults often shiver briefly. Eufala Skippers range across the Southwest, and although they fly year-round, they are somewhat scarce during winter months.

Arizona Giant-Skipper *(Agathymus aryxna)*
FAMILY: Hesperiidae (Skippers)
RANGE: AZ, western NM
ADULT FLIGHT SEASON: fall
HOSTPLANT: Palmer's agave
WINGSPAN: 1⅞–2¼ inches

Giant-skippers are large, strong-flying species whose caterpillars bore into the leaves, stems, and roots of agaves and yuccas. Populations of the Arizona Giant-Skipper are found around colonies of Palmer's agave in desert grassland and oak woodland. In general, agave-feeding giant-skippers tend to occur in tight colonies and are not prone to wander. Adults do not visit flowers, but males will attend mud. Like other members of the genus Agathymus, females lay their eggs singly on leaves of the hostplant, but the eggs do not adhere, and drop into crevices of the plant. The caterpillars bore into the leaves of the host, constructing a trapdoor through which the adult will eventually emerge.

California Giant-Skipper
(Agathymus stephensi)
FAMILY: Hesperiidae (Skippers)
RANGE: CA
ADULT FLIGHT SEASON: fall
HOSTPLANT: desert agave
WINGSPAN: 1⅞–2¼ inches

Some giant-skippers species are closely tied to a single kind of agave and often live in remote areas. Such is the case of the California Giant-Skipper, whose only home is in the boulder-strewn hills and rugged desert canyons in and around the western edge of the Anza-Borrego Desert State Park in California. Despite their limited range, these adults can be locally common in stands of desert agave. Males patrol hillsides using agave stalks and other vantage points to find females. Adults have been found to roost on small desert trees and shrubs at night, their gray undersides revealed in the glow of a lantern or flashlight.

Mary's Giant-Skipper *(Agathymus mariae)*
FAMILY: Hesperiidae (Skippers)
RANGE: NM to TX
ADULT FLIGHT SEASON: fall
HOSTPLANT: lechuguilla agave
WINGSPAN: 1½–1¾ inches

In the arid limestone hills of southeast New Mexico and west Texas, one may happen upon Mary's Giant-Skipper. Intimately associated with colonies of lechuguilla agave, this species is difficult to observe, for its haunts are naturally fortified by rough terrain and thorny plants. Males typically perch on low shrubs or rock faces, with their heads skyward.

Yucca Giant-Skipper *(Megathymus yuccae)*
FAMILY: Hesperiidae (Skippers)
RANGE: CA to TX (also eastward to GA)
ADULT FLIGHT SEASON: spring
HOSTPLANT: yuccas
WINGSPAN: 2–2½ inches

Yucca Giant-Skippers are interesting creatures. Their strong, stout bodies are equipped with strong wing muscles that enable them to fly at high speeds. Yet they feed at neither flowers nor mud, their brief adult life sustained by stored-up fat. Their caterpillars burrow into the roots of small yucca plants and feed from within, creating a grass tent through which the adult eventually emerges. Yucca Giant-Skippers are widely distributed across the region in most yucca habitats, but adults are rarely encountered. On occasion one may find a territorial male resting  at the bottom of a sandy wash or perched on the side of a shallow gully. Females flutter in and out of yucca thickets seeking healthy yucca shoots upon which to lay their eggs. These skippers have one brood in spring.

BUTTERFLY GARDENING

· · · · · ·

Until recently, pursuing butterflies was mostly a scientific field endeavor. Lately increasing numbers of people have been creating butterfly havens in their own yards by planting butterfly-friendly plants, thanks to a proliferation of information on the subject in articles, pamphlets, books, and on the Internet.

We are blessed with great butterfly diversity in the Southwest, where many species fly year-round. A number of these can be lured into your yard without using a lot of space and at little cost. An effective butterfly oasis can be created by integrating a few choice nectar sources with a few hostplants for our more common butterflies. Some plants, such as fern acacia, function as both nectar source and hostplant. Devoting more space to either of these resources will attract more butterflies to your garden.

NECTAR It is advisable to have some nectar available for as much of the year as possible. Integrate long-blooming plants with those that provide seasonal flowers. A liberal use of the best nectar plants is more favorable than using a variety, as some nectar plants will out-compete others in a garden setting. A number of desert-adapted nectar sources work well and also use less water. It is worthwhile to visit a good local butterfly garden to see what works and what doesn't. Some good nectar plants for the Southwest include:

lantana (*Lantana camara*)
butterfly mist (*Ageratum corymbosum*)
verbena (*Glandularia gooddingii,* formerly *Verbena gooddingii*)
indigo bush (*Dalea* sp.)
Texas kidneywood (*Eysenhardtia texana*)
sweet bush (*Bebbia juncea*)
bee bush (*Aloysia gratissima*)
milkweed (*Asclepias* sp.)
seepwillow (*Baccharis glutinosa*)
queen's wreath vine (*Antigonon leptopus*)

HOSTPLANTS A good sprinkling of hostplants will not only bring in more butterflies but also will create an opportunity to observe a number of different life cycles at close range. Be prepared for holes in leaves and the occasional missing flower—minor nuisances compared with the rewards of backyard butterfly watching. Some excellent hostplants include:

passion vine (*Passiflora* sp.)

senna (*Senna* sp.)

Arizona jewelflower (*Streptanthus carinatus*)

velvet mesquite (*Prosopis juliflora,* formerly *Prosopis velutina*)

milkweed (*Asclepias* sp.)

fern acacia (*Acacia angustissima*)

pipevine (*Aristolochia watsonii*)

indigo bush (*Dalea* sp.)

tansymustard (*Descurainia pinnata*)

Arizona jewelflower (*Streptanthus arizonicus*)

Palmer's Metalmarks on queen's wreath vine (Antigonon leptopus)

CONSERVATION

· · · · · ·

Future generations will be challenged to preserve the tremendous butterfly diversity in the Southwest. There are currently no threatened or endangered butterfly species in our region; however, butterflies are quite sensitive to sudden changes in their environment, and a number of factors can adversely affect their populations. The number-one threat to butterflies is the loss of habitat due to human encroachment. A few butterfly species elsewhere have been lost in this manner, and reintroduction attempts have been only partially successful. Human expansion requires water, and without proper management, our treasured wetlands will continue to dry up as water tables are lowered. The loss of these areas will adversely affect butterflies unique to those habitats.

Pesticide use, even though not directly intended for butterflies, can be lethal, especially to caterpillars. This includes indiscriminant roadside spraying as well as simply using bug spray in and around the home. Of special concern is the proliferation of invasive, exotic plants and grasses that displace the native flora that butterfly caterpillars need to survive. For example, buffelgrass (*Pennisetum ciliare*) is an aggressive exotic that threatens to take over vast portions of the Sonoran Desert.

Wildfires—while historically beneficial for butterflies because they help restore balance to local ecosystems—are now becoming hotter and more uncontrollable due to twentieth-century land-management policies regarding fire suppression, thereby posing a threat to some local, montane butterfly populations.

It has long been thought that collecting has an effect on butterflies, although there is really no concrete evidence to support this belief. In fact, automobiles on our highways kill more butterflies annually than are in all the world's insect collections combined.

Granted, change is inevitable. But radical, sudden change to our natural environments by humans is unnatural and detrimental to our native flora and fauna. So what can one do? Try supporting one or more of the many conservation organizations dedicated to preserving natural habitats. Join local groups dedicated to removing invasive plants. At home, use low-water butterfly-friendly plants. Avoid using pesticides when possible. Become familiar with some of our more common butterflies and try to educate your friends and neighbors. Perhaps they too will become passionate enough about butterflies to get involved in their preservation.

GLOSSARY

· · · · · ·

Abdomen The part of a butterfly's body farthest from the head, connected to the thorax and primarily used for reproduction.

Alkaloids Poisonous compounds found in certain plants.

Antennae A pair of sensory organs arising from the top of the adult butterfly's head.

Apiculus The small thin tip at the end of a skipper antenna.

Bask To position wings so as to gain the sun's warmth or to thermoregulate.

Brood A generation of butterflies usually on the wing during a compact timespan.

Canopy The cover provided by leaves on a tree (or trees).

Cell An area on either forewings or hindwings that is entirely enclosed by veins.

Chevron V-shaped mark.

Chitin A tough, protective substance that is the primary component of the exoskeleton.

Cienega A wet, marshy area usually not connected to a stream.

Cocoon A protective outer covering of silk that protects a pupa, usually found in moths and some skippers, but not in most other butterflies.

Colony A group of plants or animals growing or living together.

Compound eye The visual organ found in butterflies and other insects that consists of one to thousands of tiny independent photoreception units that, in turn, consist of a cornea, lens, and cells that distinguish brightness and color.

Costa The leading edge of both the forewing and the hindwing.

Costal fold A pocket of scent scales on the costa of the forewing, found on some spread-wing skippers.

Cryptic Colored and/or shaped for concealment.

Crysalis *see* Pupa.

Diapause A physiological state of dormancy whereby metabolism is reduced and reproduction is suspended, usually in response to environmental stimuli that precede unfavorable conditions. In butterflies and other insects diapause occurs during a genetically determined stage of metamorphosis.

Dimorphism The occurrence of two types of individuals in a species, distinct in coloring, size, etc; dimorphism is often a sex difference but may also be a seasonal one.

Dorsal The upper or top surface (as of a butterfly wing); relating to or near the back surface of an animal.

Exoskeleton The hard, outer shell of a butterfly that provides it protection (*also see* Chitin).

Flight season The time during which butterflies are "on the wing," or adults.

Forewing The wing of a butterfly closest to its head.

Frenulum A hook-like structure that holds the wings of moths together during flight.

Fringe Hair-like scales found along the wing margin.

Head The part of the butterfly containing the eyes, antennae, and feeding parts, to which the thorax is attached.

Herbivore An animal or insect that feeds on plants.

Hibernaculum A protective case used by some butterfly caterpillars for diapause.

Hilltopping The mate-locating behavior exhibited by males of certain butterfly species, defined by a constant patrolling of a hill or mountain summit.

Hindwing The wing of a butterfly closest to its tail.

Hostplant The plant that the caterpillar feeds on.

Hybridization The producing of offspring from two different butterfly species.

Influx A mass arrival or incoming of butterflies, often seasonal in nature.

Instar One of the stages between molts of a caterpillar.

Jet plane The basking position of most grass skippers, where the forewings are angled upward and the hindwings are held out flat.

Legume A plant in the pea family.

Lepidoptera The order of insects that includes butterflies and moths.

Local A population of butterflies restricted to a small geographical area; localized.

Margin The edge of a wing.

Molt The shedding of a caterpillar's skin to allow further growth.

Monsoon A wind system that brings moisture into the Southwest in midsummer.

Montane Pertaining to the mountains.

Müllerian mimicry A situation wherein two or more species have very similar warning signals and share genuine anti-predation attributes.

Oviposition Egg-laying by insects.

Palpus One of two facial structures (palpi) projecting on either side of the proboscis.

Parasites Usually small wasps or flies that lay their eggs inside butterfly eggs or caterpillars, eventually killing the butterfly and releasing young wasps or flies instead.

Pheromones Sex-attractant chemicals, produced in butterflies by scent scales.

Polyphagous Able to eat a variety of plants.

Proboscis The double straw-like tube through which adult butterflies obtain nectar and other nourishment.

Puddle party Assemblages of butterflies (mostly males) at mud sites.

Pupa The third stage of a butterfly's life cycle, also called a chrysalis.

Pupation The transformation from caterpillar to pupa.

Range Defines the known breeding territory of a given species.

Riparian Pertaining to the edges of rivers and creeks.

Scintillants Metalmark butterflies with metallic flecks and spots.

Stigma A sharply defined patch of scent scales found on some grass skippers and some hairstreaks.

Stray A butterfly that wanders far from its place of origin.

Submargin Wing area just inside the margin.

Subspecies A group or population of a given species that is distinguishable by color, pattern, or structure, and owing its uniqueness to isolation, climate, or geographical location.

Subtropical Of or pertaining to a loosely defined region bordering the Tropics.

Thermoregulation The process of warming by orienting the wings for maximum exposure to the sun.

Thorax The middle part of a butterfly, to which the wings are attached.

Understory Plants growing under the canopy of trees.

Ventral The underside (as of a butterfly's wing); the anterior surface, opposite the back.

SUGGESTED READING

......

Bailowitz, Richard, and Douglas Danforth. *Seventy Common Butterflies of the Southwest.* Tucson, AZ: Southwest Parks and Monuments Association, 1997.

Bailowitz, Richard A., and Jim P. Brock. *Butterflies of Southeastern Arizona.* Tucson, AZ: Sonoran Arthropod Studies, Inc., 1991.

Brock, Jim P., and Kenn Kaufman. *Butterflies of North America.* New York: Houghton Mifflin, 2003.

Glassberg, Jeffrey. *Butterflies Through Binoculars: The West, A Field Guide to the Butterflies of Western North America.* New York: Oxford University Press, 2001.

Heath, Fred, and Herbert Clarke. *An Introduction to Southern California Butterflies.* Missoula, MT: Mountain Press Publishing Co., 2003.

Monroe, Lynn. *Butterflies & Their Favorite Flowering Plants: Anza-Borrego Desert State Park & Environs.* Lyons, CO: Merryleaf Press, 2004.

INDEX OF FEATURED SPECIES

· · · · · ·